"It is no longer a question of whether or not we should set aside some more of the yet remaining native California landscape as 'breathing space'...if we do not, we will leave our children a legacy of concrete treadmills leading nowhere except to other congested places like those they will be trying to get away from."

—Former Congressman Clem Miller
Author of legislation to create
Point Reyes National Seashore

EXPLORING POINT REYES

by Phil Arnot & Elvira Monroe

A Guide to Point Reyes National Seashore

REVISED EDITION

— Preface by Paul McHugh —

Wide World Publishing/Tetra

cover photograph by Phil Arnot.   Arch Point Overlook
interior photographs by Phil Arnot

Wide World Publishing/Tetra
P.O. Box 476
San Carlos, CA 94070

Printed in the United States of America

First printing 1976
Seventh Edition 1998

ISBN: 0-884550-15-0

Library of Congress Cataloging-in-Publication Data

Arnot, Phil.
    Exploring Point Reyes.

    Includes index.
    1. Hiking—California—Point Reyes National Seashore—
Guide Books. 2. Backpacking—California—Point Reyes National
Seashore—Guide-books. 3. Trails—California—Point Reyes Nation-
al Seashore—Guide-books. 4. Point Reyes Natonal Seashore (Calif.)
I. Monroe, Elvira. II. Title.
GV199.42.C22P643   1998   917.94'62   98–5783

ACKNOWLEDGEMENTS

We would like to express appreciation to—

Don L. Neubacher
Superintendent
Point Reyes National Seashore

The Rangers, who through the years have provided us with information and articles which we have quoted and reproduced in part

and most especially

John Dell'Osso
Chief of Interpretation
Point Reyes National Seashore

Mía Monroe
Site Supervisor
Muir Woods National Monument

for their encouragement, support and assistance with technical data and provision of resource materials and current information.

Bass Lake viewed from the Coast Trail.

TABLE OF CONTENTS

Arch Rock Overlook—looking south toward Double Point.

SUPERINTENDENT'S MESSAGE

When President John F. Kennedy signed legislation to author the establishment of Point Reyes National Seashore on September 13, 1962, he knew the importance of saving and protecting a portion of the diminishing undeveloped coastline of the United States. Because of his foresight and the work of many individuals, a place of spectacular beauty is preserved forever.

Today, the coastal sanctuary of Point Reyes is one of the most visited national parks in the country. The park is world renowned for scenic vistas, and provides a home to thousands of plants and animals, including 60 at-risk species.

Along with over 60 species of mammals and 450 species of birds, the park offers nearly 150 miles of hiking trails, sweeping scenic vistas, beaches, and rugged coastline. Enjoy your visit and help the National Park Service to carefully protect the cultural and natural resources of this magnificent National Seashore. With your help, we will do our best to be stewards of these precious resources.

As John Muir once said, "Everybody needs beauty as well as bread, a place to play in and pray in, where Nature may heal and cheer and give strength to body and soul."

Don L. Neubacher
Superintendent
Point Reyes National Seashore

Double Point along WIldcat Beach

PREFACE

You can stand atop pinnacles of rock at Tomales Bluff on Point Reyes' north end as on the prow of a ship. Fresh breeze will lift your hair, the broad, gleaming wrinkles of the sea will spread out to the horizon, and seabirds screech and wheel about you like raucous, errant angels.

But in many ways, the voyage of Point Reyes is more ponderous and profound than that of any great ship. And make no mistake about it: this vast peninsula is in fact under sail, just like a vessel with a 70,000-acre main deck. (Um, would that make 1,407 foot-high Mt. Wittenberg the bridge?).

At the stately, majestic pace of two inches per year, Point Reyes is engaged in cruising north to Alaska. The peninsula, ostensibly joined to mainland Northern California, is actually separated from it by the slippery San Andreas Fault. The huge mass of Point Reyes has already glided northward some 300 miles. Ancient granite of its bedrock at one time was located in the vicinity of the present-day Tehachapis.

That's only one of the magical pieces of data about Point Reyes which help bestow upon the place a compelling allure. Another is its hairsbreadth escape from development, achieved when President Kennedy signed enabling legislation for a new National Seashore on September 13, 1962.

Now all Americans -- and quite an impressive array of wildlife -- can take a deep breath and relax into the beauty and timelessness of a relatively pristine natural scene as they roam these beaches, forests and hills.

The first important questions are, how do you start, and where should you go? That's where mountaineer, guide and author Phil Arnot comes in. This native Californian has hiked Point Reyes from stem to stern for decades, discovering all of its main features as well as many secret passageways, and written with great clarity and precision about his findings.

What you hold in your hand is the latest version of "Exploring Point Reyes" — the seventh edition, if I am not mistaken. That means Arnot has been perfecting his message about this national treasure for 22 years, constantly updating his understanding, and passing his accumulation of experiences, directions and lore onto you. It is not an excessively grandiose statement to say that the result is an invitation to discovery and adventure. Point Reyes not only provides such things in abundance, the place also presents quiet and subtle charms as well. Sometimes wreathed in mist, sometimes bathed in sunlight, the site always strikes me with something fresh and new, even if I'm hiking a trail I've seen many times before. And I have Phil Arnot to thank for deepening my experience by steering me to some spots I'd never seen, magical spots I might not have found on my own.

I'm thinking now of one long trek I made with his book in my backpack, down sand exposed by super-low tide, from Limantour to that stretch of wonders he calls Secret Beach. In reaching this place, one passes through narrow, rocky gates just like a privileged outlaw riding into the legendary Hole-in-The-Wall. Once there, banded rock, hidden nooks, pristine beach, glittering sea are all displayed for your appreciation like an outdoorsman's fantasy of ultimate beauty. One doesn't need to come upon many finds like that to start feeling large amounts of gratitude for Mr. Arnot and his endeavors. As you peruse the cornucopia of 140 miles of hiking trails described in this book, and check the helpful data on lodging and other visitor resources, its easy to feel your mind start to wander. You start wondering what visiting this or that charming feature is going to be like, and then lust to do it begins to consume all plans for the weekend. My advice: let it. And then permit your feet to follow. Finally, once on site, quaff deeply of the restoration and recreation, but also permit inspiration to occur. It took a long struggle by many people to get Point Reyes preserved as a National Seashore. This area yet needs the care of visitors, and the loving work of volunteers. But many other preservation projects and environmental endeavors in other places would also benefit from your support. Point Reyes itself may not be the only great thing that moves. The inspiration it provides can travel as well.

Paul McHugh
San Francisco Chronicle

What is the Point Reyes experience?

… a meal or a snack at one of the excellent local places after a day of hiking… a bed & breakfast stay …

... picnicking, biking, riding ...

... shopping at the local boutiques and stores...

...learning about the park from rangers at the Visitor Center...

*...whale watching
at the lighthouse...*

…crashing waves,
wildflowers,
waterfalls,
meadows,
open trails …

On different visits it is different things …

different moods, vistas, climate… but always very special.

Exploring
Point Reyes

A Guide To Point Reyes
National Seashore

*We need to keep some of our vanishing
shoreline an unspoiled place, where all
people, a few at a time, can discover
what really belongs there —
can find their own Island in Time.*

— David Brower

Overview

- *How To Get To Point Reyes National Seashore*
- *Visitor Centers* • *What You Need To Know*
- *Maps* • *Climate*

Wildcat Beach

GETTING THERE

To get to Point Reyes National Seashore Bear Valley Visitor Center (Olema), under normal traffic conditions from any of the following locations, allow time as indicated. The time estimates offered here are based on the assumption that you drive on or about the speed limit.

Berkeley (via San Rafael-Richmond Bridge)	1 hr 15 min
Oakland (via San Rafael-Richmond Bridge)	1 hr 30 min
Walnut Creek (via San Rafael-Richmond Bridge)	1 hr 50 min
San Francisco (via Golden Gate Bridge)	1 hr 15 min
San Mateo (via Golden Gate Bridge)	1 hr 35 min
Redwood City (via Golden Gate Bridge)	1 hr 45 min
Palo Alto (via Golden Gate Bridge)	1 hr 50 min
San Rafael	45 min
Mill Valley	50 min
Terra Linda	50 min
Sausalito	55 min

If you plan to start from a trailhead more distant than the one at the Visitor Center, add the following number of minutes to the time chart above:

Estero Trailhead	25 min
Muddy Hollow Trailhead	20 min
Limantour Trailhead	20 min
Five Brooks Trailhead	10 min
Abbotts Lagoon Trailhead	20-25 min
Kehoe Beach Trailhead	25-30 min
McClures Beach Trailhead	35-40 min
Palomarin Trailhead	40-45 min

Once in Marin County and heading for the National Seashore, I suggest you avoid State Highway 1 from where it leaves Highway 101 near Sausalito to Point Reyes National Seashore. Instead, take Sir Francis Drake Highway, which junctions with Highway 101 at Greenbrae. If time is not a consideration, Highway 1 is very scenic. On a highway map Highway 1 appears more direct, but the highway maps don't show the many narrow winding curves. Traveling from the Bear Valley Trailhead to either Palomarin Trailhead or Five Brooks Trailhead, do take the highway *from its junction with the Sir Francis Drake Highway at Olema only.* In this stretch Highway 1 is direct, as well as scenic. Heading south for Palomarin Trailhead from the Bear Valley Trailhead, turn off Highway 1 towards Bolinas, and turn right on Mesa Road, just outside Bolinas. Mesa Road winds for 4-5 miles before reaching Palomarin trailhead.

On Sunday afternoons in spring, summer, fall, and sometimes even in winter, the southbound traffic on the Golden Gate Bridge gets backed up bumper to bumper almost as far as the Waldo tunnel from around 3:30 p.m. until 6 or 7 p.m. Take your time hiking and do not plan to reach your car until about 5 or 6 p.m. Explore having dinner in Olema or in Point Reyes Station. This will put you behind the traffic.

> When you arrive stop by the Bear Valley Visitor Center and pick up a copy of the excellent Point Reyes National Seashore Newspaper, a map and other available literature. Visit the exhibits. All will greatly enhance your enjoyment and inform you of special activities and hikes.

Public Transportation — Since transportation company schedules change from year to year it is best to call the Point Reyes National Seashore Visitor Center (415)663-1092 for the latest information. At this writing, The Golden Gate Transit Company has very limited bus service to Point Reyes National Seashore.

VISITOR CENTERS

Bear Valley — This barn-sized building provides an orientation to the park's roads, trails and general history. Exhibits provide an introduction to the plants, animals and people of this area. Resevrations and permits for backcountry camping can be obtained here. A dramatic slide program is available upon request.

• *Monday through Friday, 9:00 am to 5:00 pm*

• *Weekends and Holidays, 8:00 am to 5:00 pm*

• *Telephone: (415) 663-1092*

• *Camping telephone: (415) 663-8054*

From a distance, the Bear Valley Visitor Center blends into the surrounding meadows and forest with the overall effect of a large old barn. The Center houses a library, collection room, auditorium, offices, and 2,500 square feet of exhibits about Point Reyes.

This Visitor Center was constructed in 1983 utilizing funds from two major private foundations: the William Field Charitable Fund and the San Francisco Foundation (Buck Fund). Each foundation donated $700,000 to cover the total $1.4 million cost of the building. This 7,600 square foot structure was designed by Henrik Bull, of the San Francisco firm of Bull, Stockwell, and Volkmann.   The interior exhibits were designed by Dan Quan, of San Francisco. Fabrication of the exhibits was completed by Greyhound Exhibit Group, also from San Francisco.

The exhibits are divided into several sections: 1) physical aspects of Point Reyes, including a weather station which indicates wind velocity and direction, temperature, and rainfall, and a seismograph; 2) history of the Coast Miwoks, early explorers, ranching, shipwrecks, and the Park itself; and 3) plant and animal communities of Point Reyes.

The interior exhibits (dioramas) were constructed by Fred Funk Exhibits, who used many interesting techniques. To preserve the flora two methods were utilized. The two large trees were actually "pickled." They were first cut down and divided into small sections, then the sections were submerged in a glycerin bath for a pickling effect. Finally, each tree was reconstructed to its original form. The other method utilized for constructing plants was "vacuum forming." Leaves were fabricated from molds and formed out of plastic. Many of the animals in the exhibit are from roadway accidents, and by using taxidermy techniques, have been preserved for the exhibits. Many visitors are intrigued with the "water" in some of the exhibits. The water is actually a casting resin that was poured over a dark soil background.

Below is a list of birds and animals that you will find in the exhibits.

Birds_____

Osprey (and nest)	American Wigeon	
California Quail	Red-winged Blackbird	
Raven	Surf Scoter	
Red-tailed Hawk	Mallard	
Brown Pelican	Stellar's Jay	
Dark-eyed Junco	Snowy Egret	
Northern Harrier	Great Blue Heron	
Acorn Woodpecker	Marsh Wren	
California Towhee	Common Murre	
Northern Saw-whet Owl	Brandt's Cormorant	
Red-shouldered Hawk	Black-bellied Plover	
Northern Pintail	Turkey Vulture	
Long-billed Dowitcher	Tufted Puffin	
Great Horned Owl		
Common Egret		
Western Gull		
Western Sandpiper		
Pelagic Cormorant		
California Gull		
Dunlin		
Northern Flicker		
Heerman's Gull		
Marbled Godwit		
Brown Creeper		
Bufflehead		

Animals_____

Muskrat
Gopher Snake
Grey Squirrel
Brushrabbit
Deer Mouse
Pond Turtle
Black-tailed Deer
Striped Skunk
Woodrat
Bobcat
Sonoma Chipmunk
Mussel
Gopher
Jack Rabbit
Anemone
Raccoon
Gray Whale Skull
Black Chiton
Harbor Seal, Female
Harbor Seal, Pup
Badger
Sea Star
Long-tailed Weasel
Barnacle
Gray Fox
Mountain Beaver

Ken Patrick — Located at beautiful Drakes Beach. Exhibits focus on 16th century maritime exploration, marine fossils and marine environments. A 250 gallon salt water aquarium is home to plant and animal life from Drakes Bay. A minke whale skeleton is suspended from the ceiling. Drakes Beach Cafe is next door.

- *Closed weekdays*
- *Weekends and Holidays, 8:00 am to 5:00 pm*
- *Telephone: (415) 696-1250*

Lighthouse — Located on the Point Reyes Headlands, the center has exhibits on whales, wildflowers and lighthouses. It is a 0.4 mile walk from the parking area. The lighthouse is 300 steps down the cliff from the visitor center. Dress warmly, weather conditions are unpredictable.

- *Open Thursday-Monday, 10:00 am to 5:00 pm*
- *Lighthouse Stairs: 10:00 am to 4:30 pm*
- *Closed Tuesday and Wednesday*
- *Telephone: (415) 669-1534*

WHAT YOU NEED TO KNOW

Hiking — The National Seashore has over 140 miles of hiking trails. Customize your hike to accomodate your physical and time limitations. Explore coastal or forest ecosystems Hike flat or strenuous terrain. To keep your adventure safe and enjoyable, and protect park resources, please observe these regulations:

- Stay on trails to avoid poison oak, stinging nettles and ticks. Do not shortcut switchbacks. This causes erosion and damages trails.

- Stay away from cliff edges. Loose soil can give way suddenly, sending you crashing to the rocks below. Do not climb cliffs.

- Dress appropriately. Wear layered clothing and be prepared for wind, rain, fog or sunshine.

- Always carry water and some food for longer hikes. Dehydration is a common cause of exhaustion, fatigue and headaches. Do not drink from streams: the protozoan *Giardia lamblia* may be present and can cause severe illness. Drinking water is available only at the visitor centers. Water at campgrounds needs to be treated.

- If horses are passing on the trail, step to the downhill side, greet the rider so the horse knows you're there. Do not touch the animals.

- There are no lifeguards on duty at any of the beaches at Point Reyes National Seashore. Severe rip currents exist along North and South Beaches, and sneaker waves can knock you down without notice. Average water temperature is 55 degrees.

Dogs — Pets are wonderful animals that give comfort and companionship. However, a national park is not the best place for them. Dogs may chase, scare and can transmit diseases to wild animals. The "scent of a predator" dogs leave behind can also disrupt or alter behavior of the native animals this park has been set aside to protect.

If you bring a dog, please observe the following regulations:

- Dogs are allowed at Kehoe Beach, South Limantour Beach, Palomarin Beach, and North and South Beaches. They are also allowed in parking lots and the Bear Valley picnic area. *Dogs must be on a leash no longer than six feet long at all times in any of these places.*

- Dogs are allowed on some trails in the Golden Gate National Recreation Area adjacent to Point Reyes National Seashore. Stop by a visitor center to pick up a free flyer on dog regulations here and in nearby parks.

- Dogs or other pets are not allowed on any hiking trails in Point Reyes National Seashore. Owners not adhering to regulations will be cited.

   These regulations do not apply to seeing eye dogs.

Biking — Over 35 miles of trails are open to bicycles at Point Reyes National Seashore, and over 10 miles more in the adjacent Golden Gate National Recreation Area. Stop by a visitor center to pick up a free trail map which defines these areas. Remember safety, courtesy and respect for the wilderness while on these trails.

- When on a bicycle trail, travel no faster than 15 miles per hour and slow down around blind curves. Bicyclists yield to both hikers and horses.

- Bicycles are not allowed off-trail or in designated wilderness areas, nor may they be walked or carried while on pedestrain trails.

- Bicycles are not allowed on the Earthquake Trail, the Woodpecker Trail or at Kule Loklo.

- Cyclists found not adhering to these rules will be cited and their equipment possibly confiscated.

Camping — There are four hike-in wilderness campgrounds. A fee is charged for the required permit. Reservations are recommended and may be made up to eight weeks in advance by calling the Bear Valley Visitor Center at (415) 663-8054, Monday through Friday, 9:00 am to 2:00 pm. Permits must be picked up at this visitor center before starting your trip. Camping anywhere outside of these four designated campgrounds or without a permit is illegal.

- Each campground has pit toilets and water. Water at the campgrounds is not safe to drink. It should be treated before drinking. Do not drink from streams or lakes without proper treatment.

- Each campsite has a picnic table, a charcoal grill and a food storage locker.

- Store food securely from animals in the food storage lockers. Dispose of scraps in waste containers or carry out. Wash dishes away from water spigots. Do not feed any wildlife!

- Wood fires are not allowed at the campsite. Use charcoal in the grills or use a backpacking stove to cook.

- Quiet time is after sunset. Please respect the wilderness enjoyment of others.

- Stay within the designated site. Camping out of bounds is illegal and only destroys the wilderness you have come to enjoy.

- Hog Island is open to day use only. No overnight camping is allowed.

Fires —

- Permits are required for any beach fire ignited within the National Seashore. Permits are available at visitor centers, the dispatch office and from field personnel. The permit is free.

- Wood fires are allowed only on beaches, well away from any vegetation. They are allowed nowhere else. Wood must be brought in from outside the park or reasonable amounts of driftwood may be gathered from beaches. The fire may not be more than 36 inches in diameter.

- Before leaving your beach fire, put it out completely with water. Do not cover up coals with sand as it will only insulate the heat and be an unseen danger to wildlife and barefoot visitors.

- Charcoal fires are allowed in the Bear Valley and Drakes Beach picnic areas and the backcountry campgrounds in the grills provided. Visitors may also have charcoal fires in their own container or grill on beaches away vegetation. Pack out used charcoal.

In order to preserve natural, cultural and archeological resources within the National Seashore, no collecting of natural objects or cultural artifacts (such as plants, flowers, seeds, nuts, antlers or arrowheads) is allowed by law.

Handicap/wheelchair Access — Ongoing efforts are being made to include disabled visitors access to all buildings and programs. A copy of the Point Reyes accessibility guide is availbale free of charge from any of the Park's visitor centers. The National Park Service provides a wheelchair for temporary use by park visitors. No rental fee is charged. The wheelchair is available at the Bear Valley Visitor Center.

Shuttles — As of this writing, the shuttle service is winter only beginning the weekend after Christmas and running through the second weekend of April. It runs weekends and holidays when the weather is clear, accommodating the additional visitation due to whale watching when the small parking lots at the Lighthouse are filled up.

MAPS

Anyone hiking should always carry a map. Even hikers familiar with the area might find that a map will be handy when encountering something new and unexpected.

Topographical Maps — Four detailed maps, a 7 1/2 minute quadrangle series, are available: *Tomales, Drakes Bay, Inverness,* and *Double Point* and *Bolinas*. They all fit together to make a very sizeable map. However, one would seldom, if ever, need to put them all together on the trail. 2 5/8 inches represents one mile on the 7 1/2 minute series. Contour intervals are 40 feet. 1 5/8 inches represent 1 kilometer. You can practically pinpoint your own body on these maps. The topographical maps are all available at: The United States Geological Survey office 345 Middlefield Way, Menlo Park, California, 94025 (telephone: map sales (650) 329-4390 fax: (650) 329-5130). Cost per map is $4.00. USGS Topographical maps are also available at REI (Recreational Equipment Incorporated) stores and at some other Bay Area mountaineering goods stores. A USGS 1-48,000 scale map of all Point Reyes National Seashore is available at the Visitor Center.

Trail maps — The National Park Service has, at the Visitor Center, a fold-out map showing the entire seashore area with paved roads, visitor centers, trails, points of interest, and prominent landmarks. This map does not show topography.

*   *   *

The National Park Service has a large sign map of the entire Seashore area between Drakes Estero and Palomarin Trailhead. This map is placed at each of the three trailheads — Olema, Five Brooks, and Palomarin — and shows the names of most trails and distances between trail junctions. Trail distances from each trailhead to particular camps and points of interest are listed at the bottom of this map. The map does not show topography. The National Park Service has a smaller paper version of this map available at the Visitor Center at Bear Valley (Olema). The National Park Service also has a handout trail map showing trails, named locations, and distances. Elevation is not shown. Also available at the Visitor Center are USGS topographical maps of the Point Reyes region.

Also of interest is an oblique-view pictorial land form map of Point Reyes National Seashore and the San Andreas fault by Dee Molenaar. Historical maps are also available.

CLIMATE

Point Reyes Peninsula's climate is characterized by warm, dry summers and cool, rainy winters, similar to the type of climate that prevails on the Mediterranean. The United States Coast Guard Station, located at the extreme western tip of the peninsula, has kept weather records for at least 80 years. There is also a weather observation station at the Bear Valley Headquarters area of the National Seashore.

There are constant winds of moderate to strong velocity on the exposed headlands and outer beaches. During most of the year, particularly in the summer, prevailing wind direction is northwesterly. There is a tendency for the winds to shift to the south during the winter. The greatest wind velocities occur in November and December during infrequent southerly gales. **Winds have been clocked up to 130 miles per hour** at the Coast Guard Station on the Point, but the annual maximum wind velocity is 43 miles per hour. Winds are much lighter on the eastern side of the Inverness Ridge, but it is an unusual day that does not bring some afternoon breezes to Point Reyes.

Headlands and beaches on the Pacific Coast are subjected to frequent heavy fogs. During most of the year, the water temperatures near the coast are lower than that of the ocean further to the west. The cooling effect of these frigid coastal waters on the warmer moist air moving past produces fog, which blankets the ocean for more than 50 miles or more off the shore and often smothers the beaches with heavy fog, reminiscent of the "thicke mists and stynkinge fogges" Sir Francis Drake's men complained of when he visited the northern California coast in June, 1579. Such heavy fogs are most common in the months of July, August and September.

Sunshine and higher temperatures occur inland. The east side of Inverness Ridge and the beaches of Tomales Bay are sheltered from the summit of the ridge westward to the ocean, leaving sunny areas for picnicing and swimming. *Inland temperatures in the summer are often 20 degrees warmer than temperatures on the Headlands and outer coast.*

Rainfall averages about 11.5 inches per year out on the Point where the Lighthouse is located, with the heaviest rainfall coming in December, January, February and March. A few miles inland the rainfall is much greater, averaging about 36 inches a year at Bear Valley Headquarters of the National Seashore. Although there is scarcely any rain from mid-April to October, the night and morning coastal fogs condensing on the trees keep the wooded hills moistened. The moderating influence of the Pacific Ocean creates an even climate with no great extremes of heat or cold. The average monthly temperatures differ only about 28 degrees from high to low throughout the entire year.

Hiking

• Criteria for hiking classification • Conversion Table For Miles To Kilometers • Conditioning For Trail Hiking • Day Hike Equipment List

CRITERIA FOR HIKING ROUTE CLASSIFICATION

Hikes in Point Reyes National Seashore have been classified as easy, moderate, or strenuous. The criteria for placing hikes in these categories is primarily distance, and secondarily change in elevation. Yet, the ultimate criteria for deciding which distances or elevation changes constitute an "easy" hike and which constitute a "strenuous" hike is subjective. After hiking 8 to 9 miles at a 3-3.5 miles an hour pace (allowing for occasional stops to examine flower, fauna, vistas, to take pictures, eat lunch) my knee and hip joints are not sore. After 18-25 miles at the same pace with the same allowance for breaks these joints do hurt.

Criteria

Easy Hike	4-9 miles
Moderate Hike	10-16 miles
Strenuous Hike	17-25 miles

If one climbs over 1500 feet on a given hike one can move the classification up a half or a full notch on the scale. There is no single climb of over 1400 feet at Point Reyes (any place on the beach to Mount Wittenberg), but one might select a route involving a number of different hill climbs which would total over 1500 feet of uphill hiking.

Actually, what is strenuous, moderate, or easy is relative to the individual. Each person must set his or her own classification system.

TABLE CONVERTING MILES TO KILOMETERS

Miles	Kilometers	Miles	Kilometers
1.0	1.6	10.5	16.8
1.5	2.4	11.0	17.6
2.0	3.2	11.5	18.4
2.5	4.0	12.0	19.2
3.0	4.8	12.5	20.0
3.5	5.6	13.0	20.8
4.0	6.4	13.5	21.6
4.5	7.2	14.0	22.4
5.0	8.0	14.5	23.2
5.5	8.8	15.0	24.0
6.0	9.6	15.5	24.8
6.5	10.4	16.0	25.6
7.0	11.2	16.5	26.4
7.5	12.0	17.0	27.2
8.0	12.8	17.5	28.0
8.5	13.6	18.0	28.8
9.0	14.4	18.5	29.6
9.5	15.2	19.0	30.4
10	16.0	19.5	31.2

CONDITIONING FOR TRAILHIKING

Hiking is a physical activity which can be enjoyed for its own sake and/or the aesthetic pleasures found in the places where only hikers can go. There is little skill associated with the physical act of hiking, for hiking is nothing more than walking.

But hiking can become strenuous, relative to the individual, when it involves long uphills, long downhills, or long levels. By my definition, "strenuous" activity is activity which places a strain on any or all parts of the body.

Uphill hiking (especially with heavy pack and/or at high altitude) is strenuous for the average person. The most effective training for uphill hiking/backpacking for me is running. Running conditions one's legs, just as, or even more important for uphill hiking/backpacking, it conditions the cardio-vascular system.

From running I learned the three essential things one must know for uphill hiking and backpacking: pace, rhythmic breathing, and overbreathing. Pace means you walk sufficiently slowly so that your breathing is comfortable, so that you are not gasping, so that you are not forced to stop, periodically, to catch your breath. It means walking at a pace sufficiently slow that your muscles do not ache. Pacing does not mean that your breathing rate is the same as it is sitting down reading. It does not mean that you need to breathe only through your nose, as some people insist. Pace means that your walking rhythm is slow enough so that, while breathing more heavily than in a resting posture, you are yet able to keep the pace without need to stop due to breathlessness or aching muscles.

Rhythmic breathing, synchronized to one's walking pace, guarantees a continual and uniform oxygen supply while exerting. Rhythmic breathing means that the time interval between breaths is the same, that the amount of time consumed in taking in and letting out air is the same.

Overbreathing, sometimes referred to as "hyperventilating," means that one consciously and deliberately breathes a little more deeply than seems necessary while moving uphill. Too much overbreathing — too fast and/or too deep — results in dizziness. Experimentation will quickly help a person find his or her own optimum degree of overbreathing and his or her own tempo of breathing. You may find that you will tend to "shift gears" in overbreathing and rhythmic breathing — a little faster and a little deeper for higher altitudes and/ or heavier pack and/or steeper terrain and/or untrailed terrain. That is, you learn to breathe a little more deeply and at a slightly faster tempo if there is more exertion. And you learn, should you get dizzy, that you are breathing too fast and/or too deeply for the degree of exertion. In time it really becomes automatic, but one has to be patient and experiment.

Hiking on level or downhill terrain does not require "wind." A running program will strengthen leg, back, and stomach muscles, but hiking itself is probably the best conditioner for level or downhill hiking. However, most of us who work from Monday through Friday do not always have time to take a long training hike two to four times during the week. Running, which takes but 20-40 minutes to get a good workout, can, then, have an advantage over hiking as a training technique.

Hiking does place more strain on joints than muscles. A long hike places considerable strain on one's feet, toes, knees, arches and heels, so it is important to build up gradually to the point where one can handle a given distance without placing undue strain on joints and feet. Proper footgear is essential.

EQUIPMENT FOR HIKING

Hiking equipment and clothing for hiking in Point Reyes National Seashore differs hardly at all from hiking equipment and clothing anywhere whether one is out for a day or for three or four days.

Footgear is probably the most important item of equipment since most people hike only for the day in Point Reyes and do not encumber themselves with much more than knapsack, lunch, water bottle, and camera. For trailhiking in a place like Point Reyes National Seashore heavy boots are unnecessary. A lightweight trail boot, properly fitted and properly cared for between hikes is all one needs. Any lightweight (no heavier than 3 1/2 pounds) trail shoe or hiking boot, such as those found at mountaineering stores is especially recommended. Trail boots made partly of Gore-tex are light and comfortable. A sturdy pair of tennis shoes or running shoes are just as good unless one has weak ankles. Tennis shoes or running shoes should have good arch support and good heel support. Do not hike in lightweight marathon running shoes. They're too thin, lack sufficient arch support, and have virtually no heel support. Some individuals can manage with these or any inadequate footgear (I've seen a few going barefooted on the trail!), but for the sometime or beginning hiker, no!

A Recommended Equipment List For A Day Hike In The Point Reyes National Seashore

1. comfortable trail boots or sturdy walking shoes, with good heel and arch support

2. 2 pairs of cotton socks or light weight wool socks for trail shoes or hiking boots

3. knapsack with plenty of side pockets

4. hiking shorts

5. a pair of long trousers in case the day grows colder or there is poison oak

6. dark glasses, especially if you are going on the beach

7. cotton shirt or blouse

8. wool sweater and windbreaker with hood, or down parka with hood

9. Swiss Army knife

10. wool cap (optional -- good in winter or on windy beaches)

11. First Aid kit (light and simple)

12. camera equipment (optional, but highly recommended)

13. notebook and pencil

14. topographical map

15. trail map

16. extra toilet paper

17. 1 quart plastic water bottle filled before you leave a trailhead and a small snack(optional)

18. sponge rubber heel lifts (eases the stress placed on the heels by the constant pounding action during the hike)

19. sun hat (optional, except for those who burn easily)

20. sunscreen (especially in summer and spring), insect repellent (optional)

21. *Exploring Point Reyes—A Guide to Point Reyes National Seashore*

22. binoculars (optional, but essential for close up views of wildlife)

23. raingear—jacket and pants recommended, pancho OK, umbrella only for short windless hikes. Take raingear if there is the slightest chance of rain.

HINT: Dress in layers (T-shirt, long sleeved shirt, sweater and or jacket). This way you are prepared for all kinds of weather and can peel like an onion if you need to.

Stretching at Divide Meadow.

Trail Guide

In any year of heavy rains or storms, some trails may be closed. It is strongly recommended you call, check the web page (parknet www.nps.gov) or stop at the Visitor Center to check on the most current conditions.

Hikers on the Woodward Valley Trail.

The Woodward Valley Loop

• *Bear Valley Trailhead* • *Mt. Wittenberg Trail*
• *Sky Trail* • *Woodward Valley Trail* • *Coast Trail*
• *Bear Valley Trail* • *Bear Valley Trailhead*

---

12 miles

Moderately difficult

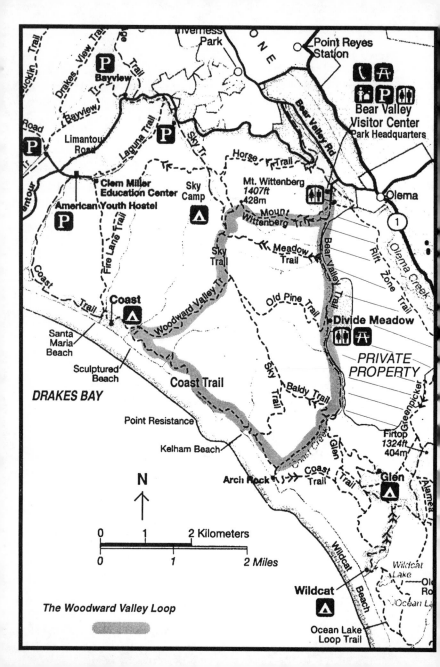

The Woodward Valley Loop

I f in a single day's 12 mile hike you want to experience sloping green meadows with lush undergrowth, rolling hills covered with wildflowers, an inspiring panorama of Drakes Bay and the Pacific Ocean beyond, open streams, waterfalls plunging over steep cliffs into the ocean, broad sandy beaches, sea caves and caverns, pelicans, seagulls, sea lions, woodpeckers, bluejays, hawks, brown deer, white deer, foxes, wildcats, chipmunks and, maybe, even a whale, then this hike is for you. In one spring day I experienced all of these things except a whale.

Try what I call the Woodward Valley Loop. You're guaranteed seeing all the land forms mentioned. Take the hike in spring and you'll have the greenery and flowers. As for the birds and animals, one can find them in any season. Only foxes, wildcats, and whales are less likely.

Setting out one spring day, I got a late start up the Mt. Wittenberg Trail from its starting point some 200 yards from the Bear Valley Trailhead parking lot. It was two in the afternoon and the day was warm and sparkling. The Mt. Wittenberg Trail begins to climb immediately, and I was soon sheltered from the sun by the groves of bay trees which arch across the trail. The warmth of the day brought out the pungent aroma of bay leaves.

In about a half mile I broke out onto an open meadow (Douglas fir are gradually invading the meadow) bordered by tall Douglas firs and gained my first view of Mount Wittenberg. The "mountain" is a high and open hill standing 1400' above sea level. From its open summit I would soon behold the expanse of Drakes Bay, sun spangles dancing on its surface on this rare windless spring afternoon.

The Mt. Wittenberg Trail skirts the summit of Mount Wittenberg and passes through a final cluster of bay, oak, and fir trees leveling off on a broad open plateau immediately south of Mount Wittenberg. From the plateau, which was covered with lupine, poppies, and tidy tips, I took the short and steep (250') trail which leads from the SkyTrail to the summit.

I had covered the 1.5 mile climb much faster than I needed to, but my late start prompted me to hurry so as to miss as little of the midday as possible. The air was sweet with the aroma of the flowers. What looked like a canary (perhaps a yellow goldfinch or summer tanager) darted past my face headed for a coyote bush somewhere down the slope. Far to the south the Olema Valley stretched straight as the fault-line which runs through its length down towards Bolinas and Stinson Beach. Mount Tamalpais lay shimmering in the sunlight on the southeastern horizon. As my eyes scanned eastward, they touched the silhouette of Mount Diablo some 50 miles away. West and northwestward the ridges of Point Reyes peninsula, alternately wooded and open, plunged westward to Drakes Bay. Between the ridges, stream canyons covered with dense undergrowth moved towards the bay. As my eyes scanned the open plateau to the south they picked up something moving in the grass — one, then two, then three blacktail deer were grazing in the tall grass near a clump of small firs. They were but 100 yards off the Mt. Wittenberg Trail which passes over the plateau. (Twice, since, I have seen a mountain lion on the plateau in midday.)

I bounded down the slope of Mount Wittenberg back to the plateau and the Mt. Wittenberg Trail in order to stalk the deer for some pictures and to resume my hike to the sea. Beyond the summit plateau the Sky Trail, an old ranch road, dropped gradually to the densely wooded Inverness Ridge. Here the Sky Trail meets the Meadow Trail, coming up from Bear Valley, and enters the stately fir forest of the Inverness Ridge once rich with an undergrowth of huckleberry, sword ferns, and other evergreen vegetation. However the Vision fire of October 1995 necessitated a widening of the trail in order to create a firebreak and most of this vegetation was removed. It is now coming back.

In about 3/4 mile I emerged from the forest into a small open meadow which stands at the head of Woodward Valley. I swung off the Sky Trail, which climbs southward and back into the forest, and turned westward onto the Woodward Valley Trail.

At this point Woodward Valley is a green amphitheater consisting of an elongated and slightly sunken lush green meadow flanked on three sides by dense dark green conifers and open at the western end. The conifers are beginning to invade the meadows. The trail moves parallel to the meadow towards the west and I was soon moving through it. Suddenly a black, red, and white woodpecker swooped gracefully above and across my path. I watched it sail on into the forest bordering the trail on the south.

Moving westward the trail began to descend slightly, then steeply, then to level off, and then to descend steeply again. Thus it followed an irregular but almost consistently declining attitude as it passed through forests, onto open hills, and back into the forest. The fire of 1995 destroyed some of the Douglas firs — mostly the smaller ones — and this becomes apparent about 3/4 mile from the Sky Trail. At one point I emerged suddenly from the forest only to behold the brownish-white cliffs at Drakes Beach. These may have been the cliffs which reminded Drake of Dover when he landed somewhere in the Bay Area in 1579.

Suddenly the Woodward Valley Trail leveled off on an open ridge, then climbed, abruptly for 50' to a hilltop. 400 yards from the sea and some 500' above it, I found myself looking out upon the expanse of Drakes Bay all the way from Double Point 5 miles south to Point Reyes itself some 8 miles directly due west. The coastline formed a giant arc which contained the spangled waters of Drakes Bay. The Farallones Islands jutted up out of the sea on the western horizon. Alamere Falls plunged ribbon-like onto the sands of Wildcat Beach far to the south. On the landshelf below, the Coast Trail contoured at the base of the hills. On the hills themselves a cluster of white deer[1] grazed casually amidst clumps of grey-green coyote brush. Blue lilac gave off its sweet aroma along the trail which fell off steeply to its junction with the Coast Trail above Sculptured Beach.

Moving on, I followed the trail, as it descended over open hills for over 1/2 mile, to its junction with the Coast Trail, about a mile from Coast Camp. At the junction of the Coast Trail and the Woodward Valley Trail one has two options.

A left, or southeast, turn on the Coast Trail will take you along the broad coastal shelf above the sea to Miller point and Arch Rock three miles from the junction and hence back to the Bear Valley Trailhead, via beautiful Bear Valley, 4.1 miles from Miller Point and Arch Rock. This route is initially level and entirely open. It offers an expansive view of the sea including, on clear days, the Farallones Islands 30 miles away. And, in complete contrast, the last four miles on the Bear Valley Trail are characterized by deep woods and occasional meadows.

---

[1] Fallow deer, native to Asia Minor and Mediterranean area of Europe. They were obtained from San Francisco Zoo by a local rancher in 1947 and turned loose.

However, I took the second option by turning right towards Coast Camp 1.3 miles away on the Coast Trail. At Coast Camp I took the 100 yard access trail to the beach, turned left, and hiked 3/4 miles south to Sculptured Beach.

The northwest end of Sculptured Beach, which I came upon just after passing some tide pools next to Santa Maria creek, is marked by a small (9'—10') southeast facing promontory. This promontory is more of a problem to hikers coming opposite to my direction. They must climb it — unless they are able to pass around it at low tide — while I had only to jump down to the soft sands of Sculptured Beach. The climb isn't really dangerous, but it involves a 3 to 8 foot climb (depending on sand depth) on a broken 90 degree face.

Once on Sculptured Beach,[2] I moved 120 yards to a short promontory (7'), climbed to a shelf atop a small and rocky headland and, since the tide was low, dropped down to the beach on the other side of the small headland and made my way for perhaps 100 yards to a rocky archway through which I passed onto still another beach. The rocky archway was simply a hole in a second truncated promontory similar to the one I had just climbed over. It is important to reemphasize that **this beach route should not be attempted except at low tide !**

On the section of beach to which the archway led, I had lunch in a sandy ampitheater surrounded on three sides by 200'–250' sheer

---

[2] Be advised that the **surf along Drakes Bay can be dangerous., especially at high tide.**

walls of fluted soil and rock. Completing my lunch, I became sleepy
and dozed off to the tune of gently lapping breakers and distant
screeching of seagulls from somewhere down the beach.

I awakened with a start and with the feeling I was being watched.
Sure enough. A pair of eyes, perched between a shiny bald head
and a straw-like moustache, was searching me from less than 100
feet away. I was being studied by a sea lion. Suddenly another head
popped up. And then another. All had probably come up from the
rookery at Double Point 6 miles down the coast.[3]

I swung onto the beach again, engaged in a short conversation with
the wary sea lions who ducked as I approached the shoreline. 300
yards southward I came upon the truncated promontory which sep-
arates Sculptured Beach from Secret Beach. To reach Secret Beach I
passed through an obvious "keyhole" in the truncated headland (safe
passage only at minus low tides) to the northern end of Secret
Beach. Passing through the keyhole I next needed to navigate some
30-40 feet of tidepools, before reaching the sands of Secret Beach.
As soon as I set foot on sand I noticed, to my left, an enormous
cave. Lowering my head, I passed under the entrance and into the
interior of the cave. The cave was well known to me, for I always
visit it when I'm on Secret Beach. Inside one finds a perfect

---

[3] During summer both **Stellar Sea Lions** and **California Sea Lions** may be seen. The
Stellar Sea Lion bull weighs from 1500 to 2200 pounds and measures up to 13 feet.
The female weighs about 600 pounds and be up to 9 feet. They are yellowish brown
in color. The **California Sea Lion** bull weighs 500 to 900 pounds, and the female 200
to 600 pounds. Both measure 6 to 8 feet. Their color is dark brown or blackish. They
are also distinguished by a ridge from the forehead to the rear of the skull called a
sagittal crest.

The best place to see both kinds of Sea Lions is the Sea Lion Overlook, located 1/4
mile before the Point Reyes Lighthouse.

miniature amphitheater surrounded by perpendicular walls leading upward to the top which is open to the sky. A perfect retreat — except at high tide!

Secret Beach is flanked by steep cliffs except for occasional creek canyons which knife through them presenting bushy escape routes difficult from the beach. Other creeks trickle over cliffs onto the sand creating, in one outstanding case, a perfect showerbath. One cannot continue southward on Secret Beach beyond the wall of Point Resistance which juts prominently out into the sea to divide Kelham Beach from Secret Beach. At the lowest of tides Point Resistance is sheer to the water. Traversing the cliff would be difficult and dangerous even with a rope. I therefore sought a way out by a cliff route with a 65-75 degree slope which *I would not recommend to anyone who has not done technical rock climbing* since the crumbly rock is 60' above the beach. Farther north, back from where I had come, one or two routes via short shallow cliffs or stream canyons can be found for those wishing to avoid exposed cliff climbing. *If you find yourself doing anything even closely resembling exposed cliff climbing, turn around, and select a safe route. Failing to find one, retrace your steps to Coast Camp or to Sculptured Beach and an access trail connecting the beach with the Coast Trail.*

My escape route up cliffs and along easy ledges brought me onto the broad shelf which stretches northwestward by southeastward above Drakes Bay and along the coast on which the Coast Trail meanders. Coming up to the trail from the edge of the cliff behind me, I could not see the trail until I came within six feet of it. It ran at right angles to me and was obscured by tall green grass.

Gliding southward along the Coast Trail, which I had left some 11.5 miles northward at its junction with Woodward Valley, I noticed more deer — this time in mixed groups of brown and white — grazing on the hills east and above the trail. I spent forty-five minutes stalking one group by crawling downwind behind them using coyote brush for a screen. I got close enough for a few telephoto pictures, but as I pressed closer the deer must have heard me. In an instant all heads lifted up and turned in my direction. For a moment they stood motionless in rapt attention. Then a white stag turned away and broke into a trot. The others turned almost as a unit and away they bounded up and through the coyote brush and out of sight. As I turned back to the trail, two wildcats swished through the grass not 50 yards away!

Farther south on the Coast Trail, which is open for its entire length, I reached the huge eucalyptus tree that marks the junction with the short trail to Kelham Beach.[4] In 300 steps I was on Kelham Beach at the point where Kelham Creek slithers down a rock face onto the beach. From the small cascade I turned and looked out on the sea to see the first of a squadron of pelicans slowly flapping northward, some 50'–70', above the breakers. A wind had come up by now and a second formation swooped down to glide just above the water and in the lee of a cresting breaker in order to gain shelter from the headwind.

Rather than return to the Coast Trail I decided to parallel it again and continue down the sandy stretches to Miller Point. There would return to the Coast Trail by way of the Sea Tunnel. By now the tide was beginning to come in and I noticed whitecaps had erased the sun spangles. Sanderlings sprinted to and fro as they moved in and out with the breakers. 3/4 of a mile from Kelham Beach I encountered Coast Creek as it glides out from under the

---

[4] Watch for poison oak along the sides of this trail.

Sea Tunnel [5] onto the beach. Getting through the Sea Tunnel required attention and concentration. I avoided the stream by traversing the rock wall on the left or north. The traverse took me only two to five inches above the water of Coast Creek. At higher tides one has to keep an eye on the breakers while heading away from the sea into the tunnel. If not, you get your feet wet which is no great tragedy but enough of a nuisance. Once my traverse was completed, I reached the cliff trail which runs some 60 yards up to Miller Point 30 vertical feet overhead.

On the Miller Point headland at Arch Rock Outlook the usual cluster of Sunday hikers were eating a snack, snoozing in the late afternoon sun, or gazing out to sea. I joined them briefly, then took up the Coast Trail 200 yards to the east as it comes down from the hills. As I moved away from the sea I glanced up at the high hills immediately south of Bear Valley Creek. Sometimes one can catch a glimpse of deer grazing on the highest ridge. Before my eyes reached the highest hill my attention was caught by a fat bushy creature moving diagonally up the shaded portion of the hillside. Had the fox remained motionless I might not have seen it. I was struck with the bushiness of the tail and the uphill speed with which it soon disappeared in some brush beneath a large cave set in a rocky cliff.

On the Coast Trail, where it junctions with the Bear Valley Trail, I joined the groups of other hikers working their way homeward up Bear Valley. Soon we'd be covered by arching bay trees and protruding fir branches. Fringing the trail, blue forget-me-nots

---

[5]At very high tides, or during storms, this should not be attempted. In the 26 years I had known the Sea Tunnel there had been a single tunnel but in April 1986 the forces or erosion (sea and stream) cut a second tunnel. Now the forces of erosion have swept away the pillar dividing the two tunnels. Thus there is now a single tunnel much wider than the first.

cheered the weary hikers. And the prickly nettle prodded those who slipped too far off the edge of the trail. In three and a half miles we'd gained almost 400' at the crest of Divide Meadow, the only

Woodward Valley Trail, just above its junction with the Coast Trail.

truly open area along the Bear Valley Trail until the Bear Valley Trailhead. In the afternoon Divide Meadow is a kind of last rest stop for hikers and cyclists. Prostrate and slumbering bodies were scattered across the pine dotted upper meadow as I plopped down for a final snack. The meadow was in shade now and the warmth of the day was quickly dissipating.

Cutting my rest short, I donned a jacket and took up the last mile and a half to the Bear Valley Trailhead parking lot. The abrupt drop from the top of Divide Meadow gave me a "running start," and in less than half an hour I had passed through the densely wooded eastern half of Bear Valley to the Bear Valley Trailhead. Emerging from the forest and into the open some 300 yards from the parking lot, I looked out upon the prominent clump of hills I call "the knuckles" (Black Mountain) as it caught the waning rays of the afternoon sun. A string of weary hikers was making its way up the straight stretch of trail to the parking lot. There was still a touch of forest aroma in the cooling air. A very special spring day was coming to an end, and my sense of joy was enhanced by my knowledge that I would come back again and again.

Wildcat Beach and Alamere Falls from the Coast Trail.

Bear Valley Trailhead (Olema) to Double Point

- *Bear Valley Trailhead* • *Bear Valley Trail*
- *Glenn Trail* • *Coast Trail* • *Wildcat Camp*
  - *Wildcat Beach* • *Alamere Falls*
- *Wildcat Beach* • *"Miller Cave"* • *Miller Point*
  - *Bear Valley Trail* • *Bear Valley Trailhead*

---

15 – 16 miles
Strenuous
Involves trail and off-trail hiking as well as about 1000 vertical feet of hiking.

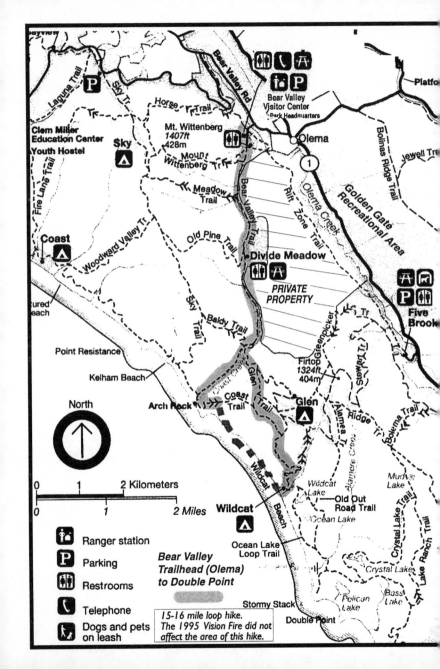

Bayview

Laguna Trail

P Sky Tr

Bear Valley Rd

Horse Trail

Clem Miller
Education Center
Youth Hostel

Sky 🏕

Mt. Wittenberg
1407ft
428m

Mount Wittenberg Tr

Meadow Trail

Bear Valley Trail

Rift Zone Trail

Olema Creek

Olema

① 1

Golden Gate Recreational Area

Bolinas Ridge Trail

Jewell Tr

Bear Valley Visitor Center
Park Headquarters

Fire Lane Trail

Woodward Valley Tr.

Old Pine Trail

Divide Meadow

PRIVATE PROPERTY

🏕 Coast

Sky Trail

Baldy Trail

Point Resistance

Firtop
1324ft
404m

Greenpicker Tr

Stewart Tr

Five Brook

P

Kelham Beach

North

Arch Rock

Coast Trail

Glen Trail

Glen 🏕

Alamere Creek

Ridge Tr

Bolema Trail

0   1   2 Kilometers

0   1   2 Miles

Wildcat Beach

Wildcat Lake

Mud Lake

Wildcat 🏕

Old Out Road Trail

Ocean Lake

Crystal Lake Trail

Lake Ranch Trail

Ocean Lake Loop Trail

Bear Valley Trailhead (Olema) to Double Point

Stormy Stack

Crystal Lake

Pelican Lake

Bass Lake

Double Point

🧍 Ranger station

P Parking

🚻 Restrooms

☎ Telephone

🐕 Dogs and pets on leash

15-16 mile loop hike.
The 1995 Vision Fire did not
affect the area of this hike.

Platfo

t was March, and broken grey clouds suggested a possible rainstorm, as a friend and I set out down the Bear Valley Trail for Double Point. Expecting to cover many miles we got off to an early start from the Bear Valley Trailhead. With packs chuck full of food, camera gear, and rain clothing we moved down the Bear Valley Trail at better than 3.5 mph.

For the better part of the 1.6 miles to Divide Meadow we strode through the dense forest of bay, fir, oak, and madrone at an irregular pace. Recent rains had left numerous puddles on the road-trail so we were forced to hop, swerve, jump, and tip-toe over, around, and through the puddles to keep our feet dry. Just as we reached Divide Meadow the sun broke through momentarily to cheer us. There was no one at the meadow — human or animal — and we stopped for a moment to listen to the silence. Then on, and slightly downhill, towards the junction with the Glen Trail, another 1.6 miles away. Soon we were back in the forest avoiding puddles and nettle on the fringe of the trail.

At the junction of the Bear Valley Trail and the Glen Trail, 1.6 miles from Divide Meadow, we spotted a cluster of lady bugs on a dead log. Then we found another cluster nearby. Then another. An entire colony with orange shells with black specs. Most of the bugs remained motionless while a few nudged upwards, sideways, or backwards but a fraction of an inch. Why the creatures had picked a location so accessible to people puzzled me. The Bear Valley Trail is the most traveled trail in the Seashore. On a Sunday afternoon in spring and summer over 300 people come and go down this trail in a single day!

Leaving the lady bugs to their fate, we started up the steep road-trail known as the Glen Trail. In 300 yards and 300 vertical feet we came upon a slanting open meadow of soggy green grass. At the fringe of the meadow a grazing white stag[1] spotted us and meandered out of sight into the dark green forest.

In an other 500 yards of uphill hiking, now out of the forest, we came upon the junction of the Glen Trail and the Glen Camp Loop Trail. We kept to the right and continued on the Glen Trail while the Glen Camp Loop Trail broke to the left towards Glen Camp one mile away. We continued upward through the Douglass fir forest. In about 300 yards we came upon a small open meadow where a now short unnamed trail (once called the Highland Loop Trail) came into the Glen Trail from the west at about a 90 degree angle. At this point we turned right (westward) onto the unnamed trail (a genuine trail in contrast to the Glen Trail, which is an old ranch road) and passed into a small but dense forest, only to emerge abruptly into open grasslands. Had we elected not to take the unnamed trail by remaining on the Glen Trail, we would have reached Glen Camp in about one mile of generally forested walking. Gradually our unnamed trail turned southwest and 300 to 400 yards brought us to the junction of the Coast Trail coming up from Miller Point and Arch Rock the sea some 800 feet and 1.4 hiking miles below.

We were in the favorite habitat of the white deer, some 800' above sea level. Here the deer feed on the lush grasslands of the open hills, and they bed down amid the clumps of coyote brush or under the fir forest east of the meadow. But the areas seemed deserted as we proceeded quietly through the green fields. Here and there clumps of wild flowers punctuated the open hillsides and sloping meadows.

---

[1] The Fallow stags have palmate antlers like moose.

The Coast Trail, which provides a magnificent view of Drakes Bay as it comes up from Miller Point, is now characterized by a broad meadow flanked by low hills covered with coyote brush to the east and a dense conifer forest to the southwest. We glided quickly through this section under gray skies and a light drizzle.

Looking over my shoulder to the northwest I saw the grey arm of Point Reyes itself jet out into the sea. It was shrouded in clouds and barely distinct. In 0.5 mile from where we picked up the Coast Trail, we came upon a "T" intersection. The Coast Trail turns right at this intersection. A left turn takes one back to the Glen Trail, which we had left 10 to 15 minutes earlier, through a conifer forest in 0.1 mile of easy walking. We turned right, or westward, still in open country, and proceeded about 400 yards to an imposing view of the sea. At this point the discontinued Old Coast Trail might be seen, somewhat overgrown, coming in from the right or northwest. Here we stood for a moment, gazing over the absolute calm of the sea far below as sunrays suddenly pierced the clouds and cast themselves on the surface of the water. We turned left or southward towards Wildcat Camp on the Coast Trail.

The descent to Wildcat Camp and Beach was spectacular. We dropped 800' in less than two miles. The view became panoramic. Some 600-700 yards from the point of our leaving the spot where the Coast Trail meets the Old Coast Trail we leveled off temporarily among some blackberry vines, coyote brush, and poison oak. To the right of this miniature and open plateau, some 100 yards away, was a group of conifers which hid, we soon discovered, some concrete gun emplacements. These had been erected by the United States Army during World War II to thwart a would-be Japanese invasion. The abandoned and dismantled forts, now covered, commanded a sweeping view of the sea some 500' below. Well hidden by the conifers, the forts were impregnable to direct assault from the beach. (The forts have since been closed up and covered with earth.)

Moving back onto the Coast Trail, we came upon an incredible view. 500' and almost directly below a road and flat meadow stretched westward to the sea with only the narrow beach between the meadow and the breakers. Wildcat Meadow (now Wildcat Camp), marked the terminus of a wooded ravine which plunged at right angles to our view. Cutting a deep canyon from the north, the ravine suddenly broadened and flattened out into the open meadow below us. Immediately south, rolling hills rose up and ran parallel to the coastline. These green hills undulated, almost totally free of conifers, until they culminated in the high hill at Double Point. The western face of this high hill fell abruptly into the sea over brownish-maroon sedementary rock. Wildcat Lake is nestled in the hills east of Wildcat Meadow. Wildcat Meadow (Wildcat Camp) lay in a kind of sunken plateau between our high perch and the 480' hill at Double Point over a mile south.

Descending abruptly towards Wildcat Meadow, we came suddenly upon another trail junction, another "T" intersection. Coming in from our left was the Stewart Trail, which originates at Five Brooks Trailhead some 4.7 miles from this point to the east. We turned right and continued downward to Wildcat Meadow and Wildcat Beach via the Coast Trail. In 1/2 mile from our junction we leveled out onto Wildcat Meadow Camp.

Dense clumps of yellow mustard flower fringed the meadow, contrasting noticeably with the green meadow and uneven grey sky. We could hear the crash of breakers from just beyond the 10' rise marking the end of the meadow and the beginning of the beach 150 yards to the west. Two black buzzards sailed lazily over the wooded hills eastward reminding me that I was hungry, so we had lunch in the meadow.

The Coast Trail brushed the southern edge of Wildcat Meadow and crossed Wildcat Creek. We followed a small trail, branching off the Coast Trail, which parallels Wildcat Creek for about 150 yards down to the beach. We wanted to get inside the cove at Double Point[2] to see if we could find some marine mammals. We could have gone back to the Coast Trail and hiked southward towards Double Point Cove, but the beach route was most direct and a safer approach to the cove. Then, along the beach route, we could see Alamere Falls a mile and a quarter down Wildcat Beach. The recent rains promised to make it spectacular.

We were soon plodding in soft sand to avoid the high tide breakers which denied us a path of hard packed sand, the kind of sand one finds at low tide. Alamere Falls and the high cliff at Double Point beyond came immediately into view as we emerged from the log jam of drift wood where Wildcat Creek meets the beach. Squadrons of pelicans, keeping 50-70 feet off the water, flew over us from the south. And, scurrying lazily away from us as we drove them down the beach, groups of sanderlings and gulls refused to be stampeded into flight.

Alamere Falls, 40' high and 15 yards wide, was full and white. Alamere Creek splashed over the falls onto the sand through which it cut a swath six inches deep and some 10 feet wide straight to the sea. From Alamere Falls one has the option of taking a side trip into

---

[2]The Park Service has since closed Double Point Cove from March 1 to June 30 because in this period seal pups are born and nurtured.

Double Point Cove about 3/4 mile down the coast. The route is difficult in one section and requires climbing on steep exposed rock 30 feet above the sea. *This side trip should not be attempted except during a minus low tide and between July and January only.* Check the tide data at the Seashore Headquarters at Olema before hand. Also, one should be respectful of the fact that Double Point Cove is the home of a large herd of marine mammals. Now that travel within the cove is restricted (it wasn't in the early days of the National Seashore) by the National Park Service one can use a fine vantage point above Double Point Cove. On a high hill (marked with "490" feet on the USGS 7 1/2 minute Double Point Topographical Map) just off the Coast Trail as it turns towards the sea at a point north of Pelican Lake one has a fine view of the marine mammals on the beach below. Only some 800 yards of uphill cross country travel over open hills is involved.

That day my friend and I decided to look at the cove so we hurdled Alamere Creek and moved, in 200 yards, to the northern tip of Double Point. We scrambled up the rock. The route required a 30' to 40' diagonal climb on a somewhat broken face to a small "platform" from which we were able to see the rest of the route. From our platform, 30' above a receding medium tide, we did a diagonally descending traverse across good rock with solid and spacious foot and handholds to the edge of a short 6 foot cliff. At the bottom of the cliff there was a large flat boulder, solid but slippery wet from the high tide a few hours searlier. We navigated the six foot cliff by searching out holds, facing in, and letting ourselves down onto the flat rock at the base. The Double Point Cove, itself still remained hidden by a narrow belt of rock lying at the base of a high cliff leads some 600 yards around and into the cove. Scrambling over a few small boulders and onto the narrow rock belt leading on towards the cove, we looked to our right to see Stormy Stack, a barren island 300 yards off-shore. It was being spectacularly pounded by the surf.

Rounding into the cove, we beheld a narrow miniature bay with a thin curve of beach connecting the far points of Double Point. The southern point, directly across from us, couldn't have been more than 700 yards away. Falling onto the beach over a low cliff was Pelican Creek. The creek ran through a narrow ravine most of which was hidden. The waters of the cove were more placid than the ocean along Wildcat Beach behind us. But nowhere in the water or on the beach was there a trace of the marine mammals who are supposed to inhabit the cove. Low breakers seemed to come at shorter intervals and churned over large grains of black sand.

We stepped off the rocky belt onto the curving beach of the northern end of the cove. I noticed a pile of driftwood strewn across the beach about 300 yards away from us and beyond Pelican Falls. We studied the driftwood. So large. So concentrated. Suddenly one of the pieces of driftwood wiggled off the beach into the sea. Then the others followed in turn. In the next minute some 75 seals slithered into the cove. Once in the water they turned, popped their heads up, and studied us from 50-100 yards.

Pelican Creek comes cascading over a 50 foot cliff onto the beach at mid-cove. Erosion has altered the cliff so much that the route has become a dangerous obstacle. Consequently, **I strongly recommend returning to Alamere Falls by the same route taken to get inside Double Point Cove.**

There are two options for returning directly to the Bear Valley Trailhead. One is to return by the same route followed to Alamere Falls from Bear Valley. This will be necessary during high tides since the northern half of Wildcat Beach will be difficult, perhaps impossible, to manage during plus high tides. At low tide one can begin the return to Bear Valley Trailhead by moving up Wildcat Beach towards Miller Point. That March day my companion and I, having returned to Wildcat Camp from Pelican Lake via the Coast Trail, found the tide medium, but fast receding so we chose a route up Wildcat Beach to Miller Point. If the tide was low we could slip through a large cave which, at medium and high tides, blocks the route to Miller Point from the northern end of Wildcat Beach. If the tide was too high, as is usually the case, we would take a cliff route from the beach to the Coast Trail (this cliff route parallels a small creek and is found about 200-300 yards from the southern promitory of Miller Point).

Moving northward up Wildcat Beach in the direction of Miller Point, we encountered magnificient cliffs of soil and rock. Here and there two and three foot piles of broken rock at the base of these cliffs reminded us of their instability. Occasionally springs came bounding down the cliffs from ledge to ledge. Perched on narrow ledges along the waterfalls bunches of yellow monkey flower were resplendent in the afternoon sunlight which had begun to break through the clouds. These seasonal waterfalls trickle down some 50-100 feet onto the beach. Abbreviated tunnels and sandy amphitheaters provided variety along the way, as did pelicans splashing into the sea onto unsuspecting fish from 100' above the water.

The tide was receding and we anticipated that the cave route at Miller Point would go. We therefore passed the cliff route,[3] marked by a clump of vegetation surrounding a spring which oozes down through a very shallow cliff. Going up the cliff route does not involve exposure to anything worse than a skinned knee, nettle sting, and a patch or two of poison oak. And in the lower going one gets sand in his or her shoes. The cliff route leads up some 150 yards and 300 vertical feet (at a 15-25 degree angle) to the old Coast Trail as it comes over the top of a small knoll overlooking Miller Point itself and to a fine view up the coastal shelf to the north. At the high point of the knoll a small headstone marks the grave of the late Clem Miller, the California State Senator whose efforts helped establish Point Reyes National Seashore. Thirty yards away you will see the current Coast Trail coming down from the hills to the northeast.

We scurried on another 150 yards along the sandy beach. The beach turned westward reaching out to form the southern tip of Miller Point. 70 yards of cautious boulder hopping on seaweed covered rocks, put us on a rocky cliff. This was easily traversed for about forty feet. A beautiful green tidepool waited to catch us if we fell. But the traverse was easy — plenty of good foot and handholds — and brought us quickly to a small hole in the cliff about 9 feet by 9 feet. An enormous log, which aided our completion of the traverse and passage through the hole in the rock wall, was jammed into the hole (the log is no longer there as of this date). Through the hole we passed to the mouth of the cave,[4] whose floor was covered with about one foot of lazily lapping water. The sides offered hand and footholds for an easy traverse into the far end of the cave which, though dripping from the recent innundation of high tide, was free of the ocean. We had no problem either in the traverse, which found us practically walking on the water, or in navigating the cave which I call "Miller Cave." Miller Cave is actually two small caves separated by a wall of rock. Both are so shallow

---

[3]This route is subject to considerable erosion during heavy winter and spring rains and may, in time, become more difficult than discussed here.

[4]The cave is impassable at high and medium tides.

they are fully lighted. Getting out of the cave requires one long step and one long reach for foot and hand holds in order to avoid a deep tidepool within the cave. Anyone who fell would simply get wet so it might be a good idea to relay cameras and day packs.

Bear Valley Trail at Divide Meadow.

Once out of Miller Cave and onto its northern lip, we traversed a low angle of rock to the small beach just below the Arch Rock Overlook (Miller Point). From there a 75 yard walk put us on the shore of Coast Creek as it plunges through the Sea Tunnel.

We stayed on the southern shore of Coast Creek, climbed 10 feet up a rock cliff, which offered generous hand and footholds, to a point where we could easily boulder hop across the creek to a trail on the northern shore and up to the Miller Point headland (commonly called Arch Rock Overlook, because of the good view to be found of Arch Rock, 100 yards off shore).

With 4.1 miles to go from Miller Point up Bear Valley to the Bear Valley trailhead, our starting point, we treated ourselves to 15 minutes rest in the late afternoon sun. Clouds cast broken shadows across the sea. A gentle wind whipped a few white caps. On the beach, 60 feet below, hikers were trudging down the sand towards Kelham Beach. I closed my eyes to listen to the muffled crash of breakers and to savour the pungent aroma of fresh spring grass.

Meadow at the Bear Valley Trailhead.

The Meadow & Old Pine Trails Loop

- *Bear Valley Trailhead* • *Bear Valley Trail*
- *Meadow Trail* • *Sky Trail* • *Old Pine Trail*
- *Bear Valley Trail* • *Bear Valley Trailhead.*

---

6 to 7 miles

Easy

Involves 1000 feet of gradual climbing through mostly forested regions.

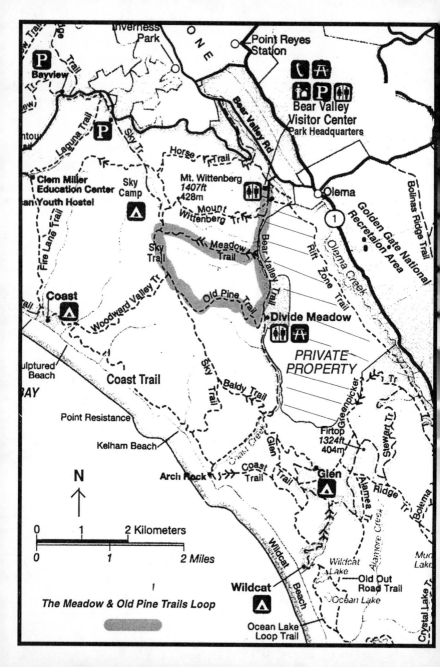

The Meadow & Old Pine Trails Loop

O rdinarily I prefer a hike which includes as much geographical-topographical variety as possible. And Point Reyes National Seashore is certainly the place for that. But for those who love the forest, or for those who want a short hike, or for those who love solitude and silence, this is the hike.

Begin at the Bear Valley Trailhead on, say a hot August morning. Go up Bear Valley (see Chapter 2) through the shade of the trees to the Meadow Trail junction 0.8 mile from the Bear Valley Trailhead. The Meadow Trail, an old ranch road which was reverted to a bona fide trail, starts up quite steeply. Arching bay trees, madrone trees with peely bark, and stately Douglas firs with grey-green beards of Spanish moss shade the route.

After less than 1/2 mile and about 400 vertical feet of hiking, I broke out onto a sunlit meadow 200 yards wide. It slanted upward at about 15-20 degrees, the average incline of the Meadow Trail. The grass is usually green here even in August, but the sun was hot this day. I longed to reach the shade at the far end of the meadow. A fir forest fringes the meadow offering shady rest spots for lunch or for quiet contemplation. One can walk off into the woods here, sit down and have the entire forest all to oneself.

Beyond the upper end of the meadow I walked back into the shade of the forest. The trail continued upward, narrow and fringed with huckleberry bushes, now ripe, and ferns. Occasionally toyons, alders, and California holly crushed in along the edges of the trail. 1 1/2 miles from the bottom at Bear Valley and 100 vertical feet up, the Meadow Trail comes abruptly on the junction with the Sky Trail. Right at the junction I found a familiar miniature meadow, fresh, green, and cool. Resisting the temptation to stop and rest on the soft green grass, I wheeled left and south along the Sky Trail towards its junction with the Woodworth Valley Trail (see Chapter 1). Beyond the Woodworth Valley Trail junction the Sky Trail rises sharply for about 100 yards and some 150-200 vertical feet before leveling and then climbing more gradually again. Then, 0.7 mile later, I suddenly came upon the Old Pine Trail junction. The Sky Trail, on which I was hiking, veered slightly right and level. I followed the Old Pine Trail up and slightly left into an even deeper forest.

I have seldom seen anyone on the Old Pine Trail[1] — weekdays or on weekends. Though the forest undergrowth is dense, one has no trouble in slipping 50-100 yards off the trail to find a resting spot. The silence is utter and the feeling is of absolute intimacy with nature. One is surrounded by a world of delicate green branches and stems. Now and then a bird flits silently from one branch to another or darts straight through the forest. On the forest floor insects climb over and under leaves, twigs, and plants in a world so alien to the world of people. If one waits long enough a group of deer may step softly through the forest enroute to some green meadow beyond. Lonely shadows cast by the trees break up patches of sunlight on the forest floor. The fir aroma is sweet in the warm air of summer and in the serenity and solitude one is lost in reveries of yesterday, today, and tomorrow.

The Old Pine Trail turns southeast, dropping at about 20-25 degrees in a few places. The total length of the trail, from its junction with the Sky Trail until it meets the Bear Valley Trail, is 1.9 miles. In the last 200 yards of the wooded trail one can hear, but not see, hikers and picnickers at Divide Meadow along the Bear Valley Trail. Then 30 yards from Divide Meadow, the Old Pine Trail breaks abruptly

---

[1] The Old Pine Trail is named for a small grove of Bishop Pines in a predominately Douglas fir forest!

On the Meadow Trail.

out of the forest and into the open. 1.6 miles eastward on the Bear Valley Trail takes the hiker to the Bear Valley Trailhead.

On the Bear Valley Trail, I dodged a pack of cyclists coming up to the meadow from the Bear Valley Trailhead and began picking up the pace for the final 1.6 miles to the parking lot.

The Meadow Trail-Old Pine Trail Loop isn't so much a hike as it is a serene and intimate experience with pure wilderness. One can hike or run through it, but to experience it takes time and a willingness to sit quietly and alone in some quiet corner of this primeval wood.

On the way to Mount Wittenberg.

The Limantour Loop

- *Bear Valley Trailhead* • *Sky Trail*
- *Fire Lane* • *Coast Trail* • *Limantour Beach*
- *Coast Trail* • *Bear Valley Trail*
- *Bear Valley Trailhead*

---

21 – 23 miles
Strenuous

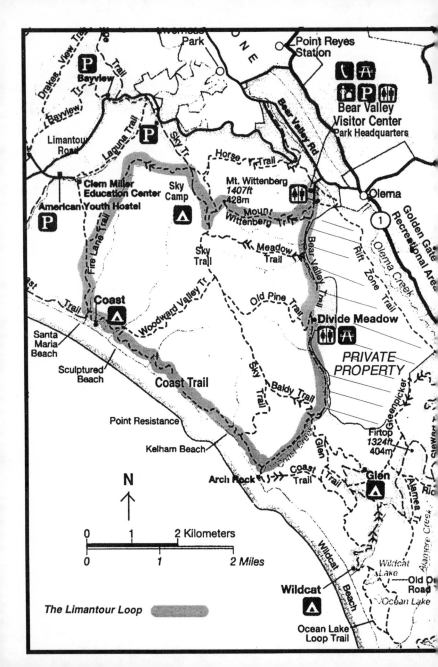

O ne April, a friend, who is a rugged hiker and climber, and I set out on a clear cool spring day from the Bear Valley Trailhead for a good hike. Our destination was the mouth of Drakes Estero on the Limantour spit. This we intended to accomplish by lunch, planning to turn around and return to Bear Valley Trailhead via a different route so as to be back in time for dinner at one of the numerous fine restaurants in Olema or Point Reyes Station. We turned off the Bear Valley Trail onto the Mt. Wittenberg Trail to green meadows, wildflowers, stately Douglas firs, the serenade of birds, and the sweet scent of the woods.

As we reached the top of Mount Wittenberg we were overcome by the glory of the day. Wildflowers were just beginning to come up everywhere — tidy tips, lupines, paint brush. The air was clean and sweet, and Drakes Bay sparkled and danced in the sharp breeze which cut across its surface. We dropped some 350' to the Sky Trail just below the summit of Mount Wittenberg. We followed the Sky Trail, to Sky Camp which is about 1.5 miles of circuitous hiking.

The meadow at Sky Camp was open, level, and commanded a fine view of Drakes Bay. We stopped for a moment to enjoy the surroundings and then took up the trail as it headed northward to a junction with the Fire Lane Trail 3/4 mile ahead. The Fire Lane takes 3.2 miles to reach Coast Camp over open terrain. After pausing for a few pictures, we moved on.

On this particular morning we saw a number of blacktail deer grazing in the meadows as we approached along the trail. The air was clean and cool which enabled us to see, in sharp relief, the brownish-white cliffs of Drakes Bay. The cliffs were some eight miles away but in the clear atmosphere they seemed closer. Whitecaps on the bay told us the westerlies had come up already. Here and there a cobweb stretched between two plant stems, sparkled with dew amid the grass still wet in the morning dampness. Clumps of iris and occasional crimson Indian paint brush broke the endless pattern of green on open ridges and meadows.

The Fire Lane took us through open country heavily vegetated with coyote brush, occasional blackberry vines and poison oak. What appeared to be a red-tailed hawk circled above Coast Camp at about our altitude (300 feet), and 1/4 mile to the west. Two white fawns (fallow deer) were already bounding away from us down the hillside when we first saw them. The deer pick up sounds and scents more readily than they see.

After 2.2 miles, the Fire Lane junctions with the Laguna Trail coming in from the north (right) and can be followed to the Point Reyes Hostel 1.1 miles away. Moving on, we found the Fire Lane developing a more gentle angle of descent in the last 3/4 mile before Coast Camp. At a large open meadow the trail leveled off and we found ourselves on the shore of a small seasonal pond on which a few ducks were swimming about.

With the sound of big combers crashing on the beach just ahead, we came to the Coast Trail junction at a point immediately northwest of Coast Camp by about 80 yards (Coast Camp itself is situated on a small meadow behind the low cliffs overlooking the sandy beach 100 to 150 yards west of the campsites via a small access trail). A sharp wind greeted us and we donned sweaters and windbreakers. Wind is the rule in springtime along the beaches of Drakes Bay. It comes up around 9 to 10 a.m., blows mildly, then gains strength in the afternoon. Usually the wind drops off and stops by nightfall only to resume the cycle the next day.

We turned northwest along the beach towards Drakes Estero five miles into the wind. Suddenly we looked up to see a flock of geese flying north 200' overhead. And then a second squadron followed. And a third. As we moved along the wind-swept beach, grey-colored willets took to flight from along the edge of the surf. They headed straight towards the breakers, then banked downwind, and accelerated on the steady blast of cold air. The single white stripe on the willet's wings distinguishes it from seagulls, which are just as numerous along Drakes beach.

We soon pulled even with the very few scattered beach houses of the now defunct Drakes Bay Estates, a housing development project arrested some years ago by the establishment of Point Reyes National Seashore. Beyond the beach homes, now occupied by park personnel, we approached the opening of Drakes Estero. We turned into the dunes for shelter from the wind and to take our lunch. We were on Limantour Spit which jets westward for 3 1/2 miles from its anchor about a mile northwest of Santa Maria Beach and Coast Camp.

Following lunch we explored the mud flats along the north shore of Limantour Spit and worked our way westward about 500 yards to the mouth of Drakes Estero. In 1579 Sir Francis Drake, according to generally accepted but not undisputed theory, sailed his Golden Hinde vessel through the mouth of the Estero for a careenage somewhere on the sheltered shore opposite us. Gazing across the open landscapes west and north, I imagined that the scene could well have looked identical in 1579. From my vantage point at the tip of Limantour Spit I could see few hints of humankind — a ranch house and a few cows were the only things suggesting human intrusion.

Turning eastward, we cut across the low dunes dividing the mud flats of Limantour Spit from the ocean beach along Drakes Bay and headed on downwind towards the mouth of Bear Valley 7 miles from the western tip of Limantour Spit. Small grains of wind bourne sand raced past us just a few inches off the beach. White caps danced wildly on the brilliant surface of the sea. The afternoon sun had moved westward so that it began to illuminate the breakers from behind. The big boomers were nearly transparent as they surged up and crested over. Each surging wall of water was greenish in color and we could see masses of brownish sand suspended in the rising breakers just before they crested and crashed. The wind whipped a fine spray of mist off the breaker crests just before they turned downward. Our progress down the beach back to Coast Camp was slowed as we became absorbed in the ocean drama before us.

At Coast Camp we left the windy beach and the stinging sand to take up the Coast Trail. Our plan was to stay on the Coast Trail all the way — four miles — to the mouth of Bear Valley rather than to alternate by moving along the beach from time to time.

For most of its length (from the Hostel, formerly Laguna Ranch, to the mouth of Bear Valley) the Coast Trail parallels Drakes Bay. The trail moves across a natural shelf between the tops of the sea cliffs on the west and the base of the sharply rising hills to the east. The trail contours to avoid deep ravines cut by four southwest running creeks between Coast Camp and the mouth of Bear Valley. We escaped the stinging sand of this unusually gusty March day, but on the exposed shelf we found no respite from the wind. Where the Coast Trail crossed the four creeks mentioned we did find shelter by slipping into the forests of bay trees which generally terminate at the point of contact with the Coast Trail. Some of the bay trees were destroyed by the Vision fire. Coyote brush and flowers have returned.

Heading southeastward on the Coast Trail, we caught glimpses of white deer grazing on the grassy slopes to our left and northeastward. And from time to time Double Point and Alamere Falls, four to five miles down the beach, came into view. As the Coast Trail passed by Point Resistance we left it temporarily to walk out onto the headland for a better view of the unnamed rock (I call it "Resistance Rock") to view the variety of bird life. The rock is the home of many seabirds, including pelicans ranging Drakes Beach. The chatter of birds which one can hear from the Coast Trail on a less windy day, could easily be heard above the wind at this point.

Then back onto the Coast Trail from the tip of point Resistance headland (200 yards) and on to Bear Valley Trail. Half a mile up Bear Valley we escaped all traces of the wind and took our first sitting break since leaving Limantour Spit some eight miles back. The hush of the forest was a welcome change from the constant rumbling of the wind. Only the faint mirthful gurgle of Coast Creek, running through Bear Valley, intruded upon the silence. With some 18 miles behind us, we especially enjoyed the respite. Then on to the Visitor Center through ever beautiful and serene Bear Valley.

*McClures Beach as seen from near the trail between
the McClures Beach Trailhead and Tomales Point.*

The Tomales Point Loop

- *Tomales Point Trailhead* • *Pierce Ranch Trail*
  - *Tomales Point* • *West Shore Tomales Bay*
- *Upper Pierce Ranch* • *Tomales Point Trailhead*

---

9 – 10 miles
Moderate

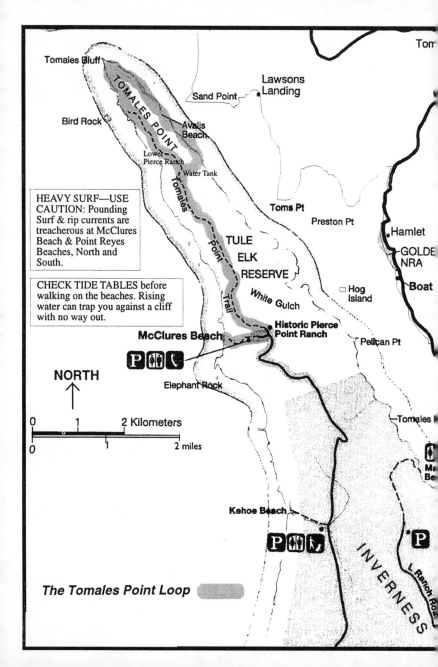

Tomales

Tomales Bluff

Lawsons Landing

Sand Point

TOMALES POINT

Bird Rock

Avalis Beach

Lower Pierce Ranch

Water Tank

Toms Pt

Preston Pt

Hamlet

GOLDE NRA

HEAVY SURF—USE CAUTION: Pounding Surf & rip currents are treacherous at McClures Beach & Point Reyes Beaches, North and South.

TULE ELK RESERVE

Tomales Point Trail

White Gulch

Boat

CHECK TIDE TABLES before walking on the beaches. Rising water can trap you against a cliff with no way out.

Hog Island

Historic Pierce Point Ranch

McClures Beach

Pelican Pt

NORTH

Elephant Rock

0   1   2 Kilometers

0   1   2 miles

Tomales

Kehoe Beach

INVERNESS

L. Ranch Rd.

The Tomales Point Loop

A t the northern tip of Point Reyes National Seashore a prominent peninsula protrudes northwestward between the Pacific Ocean and the long arm of Tomales Bay (Tomales Bay inundates a depressed section of the San Andreas earthquake fault-line and would make an island of the seashore area, as it once did, if it extended about 12 more miles to Bolinas Lagoon). A fascinating hike is to circumvent the narrow peninsula, a 10 to 11 mile trek involving trail and off-trail hiking.

On a balmy spring day a few years ago I took a group to McClures Beach, about 15 road miles from the Bear Valley Trailhead. We parked the cars at the parking area and picked up the road-trail which heads northward towards the tip of the peninsula at Tomales Bluff 4.5 miles away. We traveled on generally level and entirely open terrain, the highest point being 471' above sea level.

Occasionally we left the trail to walk 100 yards or so to the edge of the ocean cliffs facing the Pacific Ocean in hopes of searching out a beach route below. Not only were there few if any safe hiking routes down to the beach save one to Driftwood beach, but the beach below was dissected by proturding cliffs which block passage along the beach except at the lowest of tides. Subsequent attempts on my part to pass from McClures Beach to Tomales Bluff by a beach route have been accomplished only at very low minus tides. *A potentially dangerous hike.* From our cliff's edge viewpoint we observed numerous offshore rocks, many of which harbored birds and seals. The surf, which pounded these offshore rocks, was visible by the swirl of white water splashing around and, in some cases, over them.

Here and there along our road-trail, clumps of rotted granitic rock broke through the sandy soil. On such an outcrop, not far from

Tomales Bluff, we had our lunch. To the northeast the far shore of Tomales Bay was often visible as we continued towards Tomales Bluff along the road-trail which becomes a narrow trail about 2 miles from Tomales Bluff. Continuing involved hiking through open, level, and sandy terrain while squirming through numerous clumps of yellow lupine (blooms in May and June). In the spring yellow lupine covers the entire landscape in the last mile to Tomales Point. Tomales Point or Bluff itself stood less than 100' above the surf. Below the bluff a cluster of desolate weather worn rocks marked the shoreline and seemed to defy the oncoming breakers which came row upon row against them. Directly north and northwest the waters of Bodega Bay were whitecapped in the rising breeze. Far to the north tiny white dots of fishing boats marked Bodega Cove and harbor. Small offshore reefs cut across the southern end of Bodega Bay like so many giant stepping stones.

We retraced our steps on the trail for about 1 mile then turned southeast on open hills and hiked to a narrow beach (Avalis Beach) which was readily accessible. From this point the shoreline along the west edge of Tomales Bay[1] consists of a narrow beach interrupted from time to time by short rock protrusions which divide what would otherwise be a continuous beach into sections. We passed these rock protrusions, which extend from small 3 foot to 10 foot cliffs, by wading ankle-deep to knee-deep around them in calm water.[2] There was no problem with the six inch "breakers" along this sheltered shore, though some in our party preferred to wade in their tennis shoes because of occasional sharp rocks.

---

[1] It is strongly recommended that the return beach route to the Tomales Point Trailhead not be attempted in anything higher than a 0 tide. Check at the Seashore Headquarters beforehand to obtain tide information for Tomales Bay.

[2] Tomales Bay occasionally has sharks. Please be advised that you wade at your own risk.

The terrain above and beyond the cliffs consisted of gently upward rolling hills covered with brush and sparce clumps of scrub trees. The vegetation on this side of Tomales Bluff, was much more dense than on the west side and not inviting to cross country travel. Absent from view were the conifers so characteristic of the National Seashore between the Point Reyes Hostel and the southern boundary just north of Bolinas. In fact, there are few conifers anywhere in the area from McClures Beach to Tomales Bluff.

On Tomales Point Trail by moonlight.

A variety of waterbirds were visisble off-shore as we alternately walked the beach and waded in the shallow water around the rock protrusions breaking the continuity of the beach. Many small creeks originating from low gradient gullies inland, poured out onto the sands and into the bay.

From Avalis Beach proceed south along the beach for about a mile to a beach behind which there is a large and thick stand of Eucalyptus. Turn to the trees which crush right up to the west end of the narrow beach. You will find a "use-trail" leading steeply up through the trees for 1/4 mile before shallowing out in open country. Then the use-trail levels out as it heads west for about 600 yards and intersects Tomales Point Trail on which you traveled earlier in the day. Turn left or southwest towards the clump of Cypress trees which once formed a wind break for Lower Pierce Ranch (dismantled by the Park Service years ago).

It is possible — *AT MINUS LOW TIDES ONLY* — to continue down the Tomales Bay coastline from Avalis Beach to White Gulch a distance of about 4 miles. Continue south along the beach from the grove of Eucalyptus trees to White Gulch, a small bay actually. Here you must turn directly south and inland from the north shore of White Gulch.

The terrain is wooded and marshy in places (especially spring/ summer), and there are a few patches of poison oak to be circum-vented. In about a half mile you'll find an old ranch road in the trees leading right up to the Pierce Ranch site (buildings maintained and painted white) and your autos. *This route is strictly for the adventuresome hiker.* You should begin this hike from Avalis Beach starting about 1/2 hour before the minus low tide reaches its peak (consult your tide table before proceeding).

The round trip hike from the Pierce Ranch Trailhead to Tomales Point and back via the Tomales Bay coast, as described, is 9 to 10 miles. What it lacks in topographical variety it makes up for in wildlife and, in spring, one of the thickest concentration of wildflowers at Point Reyes. Sometimes whales can be seen from the Pacific Ocean side of the hills. More common are deer, foxes, numerous rodents, rabbits and, along Tomales Bay, seals and a variety of sea birds including blue herons, cormorants, gulls, pipers and others. In the early 1980's a mountain lion was sighted in the Tomales headlands north of the parking area. A pair of binoculars is recommended to give you a better look at the wildlife in this very open country.

Open meadow along the Sky Trail

Bear Valley Loop

- *Bear Valley Trailhead* • *Mt Wittenberg*
- *Sky Trail* • *Coast Trail* • *Bear Valley Trail*
- *Bear Valley Trailhead*

---

10 – 11 miles
- *1400 feet of trail climbing*
Moderate

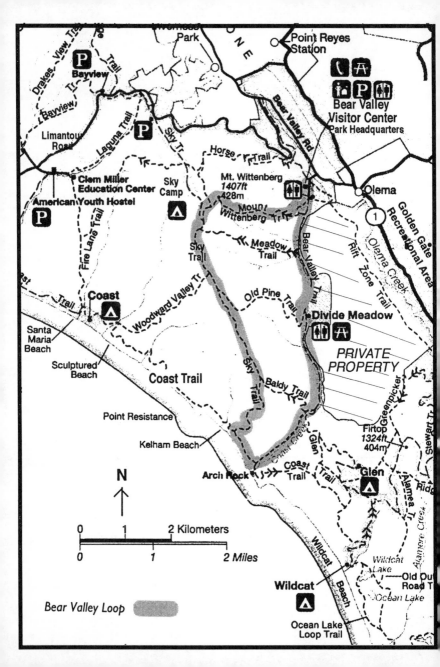

Point Reyes Station

Bayview

Inverness Park

Drakes View Trail

Bayview Trail

Limantour Road

Laguna Trail

Sky Tr.

Horse Trail

Clem Miller Education Center

American Youth Hostel

Sky Camp

Mt. Wittenberg
1407ft
428m

Mount Wittenberg Tr.

Olema

Bear Valley Visitor Center
Park Headquarters

Golden Gate Recreational Area

Rift Zone Trail

Olema Creek

Fire Lane Trail

Meadow Trail

Coast

Woodward Valley Tr.

Old Pine Trail

Bear Valley Trail

Divide Meadow

Santa Maria Beach

PRIVATE PROPERTY

Sculptured Beach

Coast Trail

Sky Trail

Baldy Trail

Greenpicker Tr.

Firtop
1324ft
404m

Point Resistance

Kelham Beach

Coast Creek

Glen

Stewart Tr.

Arch Rock

Coast Trail

Glen Trail

Alamea Tr.

N

0   1   2 Kilometers

0   1   2 Miles

Wildcat

Wildcat Beach

Wildcat Lake

Old Out Road Tr.

Ocean Lake

Ocean Lake Loop Trail

Bear Valley Loop

T hose who want the shortest possible hike with the maximum variety of terrain try this one. You'll have immediate uphill, plenty of downhill, yet mostly level hiking. In this eleven mile hike you'll have just about everything Point Reyes National Seashore has to offer.

You start from the Bear Valley Trailhead and take the Mt. Wittenberg Trail off the Bear Valley Trail. Proceed to the Sky Trail along the Inverness Ridge to the junction with first the Meadow Trail (2 miles from Bear Valley Trailhead and 1000 feet elevation) and then the Old Pine Trail (3 miles from Bear Valley Trailhead).

Beyond the Old Pine Trail junction, the Sky Trail continues its nearly due southward direction through dense conifers, huckleberries, thimbleberries, madrones, bays, ferns, and toyons on the Inverness Ridge. The first time I ever hiked the Sky Trail in its entirety, I was struck by the sudden emergence onto open sunlit hills of green grass sprinkled liberally with wild oats. And almost as soon as I broke out of the forest, 1 1/2 miles south of the Old Pine Trail junction, the Sky Trail dipped and rose sharply to an open grassy knoll. Leaving the trail and stepping 30 yards to the west, I crested the knoll to discover a magnificent view of Drakes Bay and much of the region south of Kelham Beach. A perfect lunch stop — well off the trail, with an outstanding panoramic view.

From my vista point I returned to the Sky Trail which began an increasingly steep drop. In one mile's hiking I was to drop 750' to the Coast Trail below, and most of that drop took place in the last 1/4 mile. While descending through open and rolling meadows I enjoyed an intimate view of the regions from Point Resistance to Double Point. As the trail turned westward to move into a small grove of bays and oaks, I looked to my left and south to observe a band of white deer grazing on a grassy knoll studded with tall thistles and coyote brush. Using the coyote brush as a screen, I crawled from bush to bush in futile attempts to get close enough for a good telephoto picture. I was upwind from the band and the last I saw of them they were 100 yards away and running.

Picking up the Sky Trail[1] again, I slipped through the small grove of bay and oak, emerged into the open again some 100 feet downtrail, and came upon my first view of the Coast Trail 400 feet below stretching at right angles to my line of descent. In a few minutes I bounded down onto the Coast Trail[2], turned right, and some 600 yards later reached the small footpath which leads to Kelham Beach 150 yards off the Coast Trail. Here on the warm and nearly deserted sands I stretched out, closed my eyes, and listened to the concert of the surf until I fell asleep.

After my nap I awoke to notice that the low tide had become even lower during my sleep. This gave me an opportunity to explore the large cave 600 yards up (northwest) the beach. The cave, navigatable only at low tide, was dripping from its 20 foot ceiling as I worked my way towards a small opening some 50 feet at the far end of the cave. As I progressed toward the small opening the cave ceiling became lower, and I had to crouch low to pass through the opening and onto a secluded semi-circle of beach. The beach, narrow and wet, was surrounded on three sides by the sheer walls of Point Resistence which cradles it. The beach itself was no more than 30 to 35 yards across.

---

[1]For an alternate route back to Bear Valley, take the Old Baldy Trail off Sky Trail. The Old Baldy Trail descends through the forest to Bear Valley at the junction of the Bear Valley Trail and the Glen Trail. This alternate route shortens the hike by about one mile.

[2]The Vision Fire (1995) caused a rerouting of the Sky Trail in the last 200 foot drop to the Coast Trail. The Sky trail junctions with the Coast Trail about 300 yards farther south.

From Kelham Beach back to Bear Valley Trailhead the two most direct return options open to me were: 1) proceeding down the beach (southeast) 3/4 mile to the Sea Tunnel, through the small, usually navigable tunnel, and up onto the Bear Valley Trail via the footpath just past the "inside" end of the Sea Tunnel. The foot path takes one to Miller Point directly over the tunnel and then, over open

On Sculptured Beach.

grassslands, to the Coast Trail 300 yards from Arch Rock/Miller Point. 2) proceeding to the Coast Trail via the footpath from Kelham Beach and moving southeastward in open country about one mile to where the Coast Trail breaks to the right as a footpath and the Bear Valley Trail breaks left as the same road trail. From this junction it would be 4 miles of woods and meadows back to the Bear Valley Trailhead.

Off the Sunset Beach Trail.

The Estero Region

- *Estero Region parking lot* • *Home Bay*
  - *Estero de Limantour* • *Home Bay*
    - *Estero Region parking lot*

---

8 – 9 miles
Easy

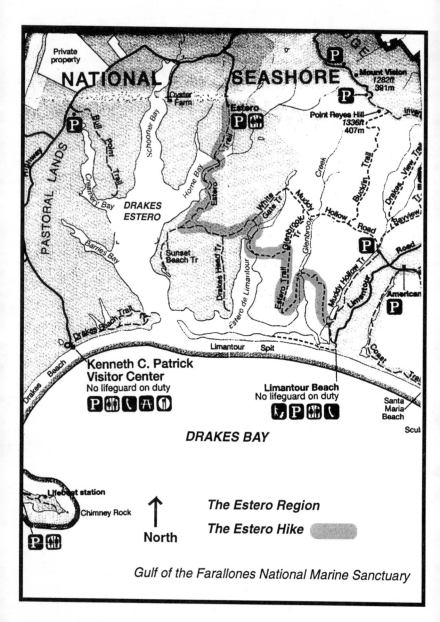

T he Estero region, situated in the northwest corner of Point Reyes National Seashore, has no broad beaches, no ocean caves, no waterfalls or natural lakes, no deep forests or high hills. Yet it is distinctive. For it has sweeping moors reminiscent of Scotland. And wildlife, abundant and highly visible—bobcats, Axis deer, Fallow deer, Black-tailed deer, marsh hawks, white pelicans, a variety of geese, cormorants, herons, and egrets. Out on the low tide sand bars colonies of seals sun themselves for an hour or two. In spring lupine, paint brush, asters, tidy tips, and monkey flower are abundant but clumps of Douglas iris are dominant starting as early as February.

There is a network of trails throughout the Estero region. They provide, thus, a variety of hikes having various distances. The main artery of this trail network is the Estero Trail.

The Point Reyes administration had recently revised the Estero Trail[1] so, needing to update this chapter and being curious about what new areas it might lead me to, I set out to do the Estero Trail twice before turning to my pen. Once in the spring and again in autumn.

I began at the broad hillside immediately west of the Estero Trail (parking lot is .7 mile from Francis Drake Blvd.) On my spring hike clumps of iris had greeted me frequently all along the 9 mile hike, whereas in fall the purple flowers were gone and the plants had turned partly a brown-rust color. The perennial coyote brush remained—dominant in scattered thickets and blossoming in fall. Easily seen in both seasons were the white Fallow deer, grazing

[1] The new Estero Trail is simply a rerouted trail using, in most cases, an old ranch road long ago put in by ranchers. Part of the region surrounding the trail was burned by the Vision Fire of 1995. But the grasslands, brush, and especially the wild flowers have come back.

either solitary or in small groups of 6 or 7. In fall I came closer to Axis deer, which confine themselves to this area of the National Seashore, more than ever before. Axis deer are characterized by white spots on tan bodies, white lower legs, and, with the stags, horns shaped more like gazelles than those of the California Black-tailed deer. On my autumn hike of the Estero Trail I surprised a bobcat which had been lurking nearby. In both seasons Blue Herons and egrets stalked the mud flats along Drakes Estero at lowtide. And in the Limantour Estero a squadron of 6 or 7 white pelicans majestically sailed high and away during my fall excursion. Cormorants, wings flapping with characteristic fury, dashed across Drakes Estero low to the water to avoid the stiff springtime winds. A marsh hawk buzzed me on the downwind during my April hike, but the two I saw in autumn were barely discernable as they soared over the shore of Limantour Estero. Black-tailed deer were frequently seen in the coyote brush in both seasons. Seagulls, of course, were constantly riding the airways of the western edges of Drakes and Limantour Esteros.

The Estero Trail — in its present condition — is no easy trail to follow. For nearly half its length it is obscure. In some places there is no discernable trail to follow — only directional arrows on posts a few of which have fallen. Therefore, some detailed description is necessary here.

The trail signs tell you it is 6.4 miles from Estero Trailhead off of Francis Drake Blvd. to its terminus at its junction with the Muddy Hollow Trail. Since many people will prefer to take this hike in one direction, having left a pick-up car at Limantour Beach parking area, you might as well consider the hike 6.8 miles one way since Limantour Beach is .4 mile from the Estero-Muddy Hollow Trail junction. It is my sense that the Estero Trail is more than the 6.4

miles indicated on the trail signs at both ends of the hike. I believe the one way distance is actually 8-9 miles. Thus, a round trip hike would be 16-18 miles if my estimations is correct. I suggest that the hike be done as a one way hike so that the hiker will have plenty of time to enjoy the scenery and, especially, the abundant bird life (10-12 marsh hawks on my most recent hike of the Estero Trail). The only problem with a one way hike is that you'll need to leave a pick-up car at which ever end of the hike you plan to finish. The hike description here will be based on the assumption that you will start at the Estero Trailhead near Francis Drake Blvd. and finish at Limantour Beach.

After leaving the parking lot at the trailhead, the Estero Trail becomes an up and down old ranch road which bridges the east end of Drakes Estero (you can watch the tide rushing in or out from the bridge). Then it climbs and dips until, 2.2 miles from the trailhead, it makes a 90 degree left or eastward turn. A trail sign informed me that if I continued straight ahead (south) I would be traveling on the Sunset Beach Trail[2] which would put me on the Limantour Estero shore in 1.5 miles of easy walking. Had I proceeded to Sunset Beach I would have had Drakes Estero almost constantly in view to my right (west). And a small, usually deserted, sandy beach nestled between cliffs rising sheer out of the waters of Limantour Estero. However, I chose the Estero Trail and turned left onto what is the semi cross country section of the route. Moving, thus, in an eastward direction and up a gently rising grass slope I found no discernible trail. Then, in about 100 yards from the junction just behind me, I came upon a simple post with a white

---

[2] The Sunset Beach Trail was once part of the original Estero Trail.

directional arrow on a blue background directing me to a turnstile in a fence where there is a concrete water pond, a directional arrow and a trail sign reading: "Drakes Head Trail .06 miles, Glenbrook Trail 2.0, and Muddy Hollow Trail 4.0 [3]. I saw a large metal water tank about 400 yards ahead and to my right. I passed through the turnstile and followed the trail for a short distance to another fence running at right angles to me. Here there was a second turnstile to pass through. The large metal water tank was now about 90 degrees to my right and about 200 yards away. I continued about 100 plus yards to still another fence running at right angles to the trail. Here there was a third turnstile, a kind of corral, and a small concrete water pond (may or may not have water in it). I passed through the turnstile and saw a partly obscure directional trail sign about 70 yards down along the fence line paralleling me on the left. Here there was a fourth turnstile to pass through by turning left or somewhat northeastward. The trail now became obscure. I walked about 50 yards away from the fence in a northeasterly direction and found the trail descending towards the west shore of the large south-north running inlet of Limantour Estero.

Once the trail had come close to the west shore of the Limantour Estero inlet described above I found it turning briefly northward in first a dike and then along a shelf some 50 feet above the marsh situated just north of the dike. As I moved up onto the land bridge (a body of fresh water on my left or north), I saw a trail sign just to my left[4]. The sign marks[5] the White Gate Trail, a seldom used trail 0.9

[3]A fine detour, or separate hike in itself, is to hike on out to Drakes Head bluff. The ranch road/trail takes you towards a clump of conifers about 3/4 mile from the trail junction at the turnstile (again, I think the trail sign is inaccurate). The country is open and quite similar to the Scottish moors. Just about a half mile beyond the conifers an old cow path takes you to the edge of the bluff overlooking the Limantour Estero, the cliffs of Drakes Beach, and much of Drakes Bay itself. From the bluff I have, on past occasions, retraced my steps some 200-250 yards to descend, northward, to a very private beach situated immediately west of the Drake Head itself. A round trip from the Estero Trailhead to Drakes Head and back is about 8-9 miles across sweeping moors.

mile in length to where it meets the Muddy Hollow Road. At This junction there is a trail sign giving directions to destinations and mileages. Incidentally, one can deviate from Estero Trail at this point, as I have done, and take the White Gate Trail, which veers right shortly after the trail sign, to the Muddy Hollow Road. Then follow that road trail for .5 mile to the Glenbrook Trail, from where there are sweeping vistas in all directions, and turn south for .7 mile to the Estero Trail. This deviation will take you past a large inland lake full of bird life along the White Gate Trail, one can expect numerous marsh hawks, ducks, a few cormorants, and an occasional blue heron. On this day I did not take the deviation but followed across the land bridge to find Estero Trail turning south along the east shore of the Limantour Estero's north-south running inlet. Here the trail was quite overgrown (at this writing it is not maintained), but I did not encounter a true bushwack and there was very little poison oak. Some prefer the White Gate deviation mentioned above primarily to avoid this 800 yard section where the trail is overgrown.

I now found the Estero Trail turning northeastward, upward, and away from the estero. As it did so it evolved from a bona fide trail into an old ranch road. Then, in about 600-800 yards, I came upon the junction of the Estero Trail and the Glenbrook Trail coming down from my left (north). At this junction the Estero Trail turned directly south for about a half mile in open country.

Moving along I could see the sands of Limantour Beach across Limantour Estero. To the west the cliffs of Drakes Bay rose sheer

---

[4] If coming from Limantour Beach to the Estero Trailhead near Francis Drake Blvd. keep to the left most of three closely parallel paths and follow the trail as it leads to a small foot bridge to continue along the west shore of the Limantour inlet. DO NOT take a 90 degree right and go up a steep, well marked cow path.

[5] Be alert trail signs and the aforementioned signs with directional arrows collapse during heavy rains and/or winds.

and bright in the brilliant light of spring but dull and somber on the foggy day of my mid October hike. In 800 yards I found the trail gradually turning me 180 degrees. Thus I was soon heading north instead of due south. The Estero Trail is the most circuitous trail in Point Reyes National Seashore. No sooner had I made the sweeping change in direction on my autumn hike but a bobcat, startled by my sudden approach, bounded across the grass. It had apparently been eating the carcass of a recently dead Black-tailed stag. Beyond the dead deer I came upon a grove of eucalyptus, partly destroyed by the fire, looking very much out of place here on the coyote brush covered moors.

At Drakes Beach

The trail now turned east through a marsh and alder thicket. Then, catching me off guard, the path turned 90 degrees left, or north, immediately past the bridge which crosses the wettest part of the marsh. Following the trail, I entered it into the alder thicket for about 100 yards before breaking out, again, in open country. The Estero Trail then began a winding climb up a 300 foot hill to a broad and flat summit. Fully in view, now, were Muddy Hollow and the fresh water pond at its western terminus. The pond is separated from the Limantour marsh lands by a land bridge. Numerous ducks, startled by my sudden emergence from the alders surrounding the land bridge, fluttered and flapped away in a rising formation. A Blue Heron, however, chose to ignore me from but 70 yards away. Then, in .4 mile, I came abruptly upon Limantour Beach parking lot to complete a 9 mile hike across the bush covered moors of the unique Estero region.

For those accustomed to the forested and rugged coastal areas typical of central and southern Point Reyes National Seashore the Estero Region offers a considerably different environment which is lightly traveled and possessing highly visible wildlife.

Mud Lake on the Lake Ranch Trail.

The Five Brooks —
Lake Ranch Loop

• *Five Brooks Trailhead* • *Stewart Trail*
• *Greenpicker Trail* • *Stewart Trail* •
Coast Trail • *Lake Ranch Trail*
• *Bolema Trail* • *Olema Valley Trail*

---

14 – 15 miles
Moderate – Strenuous
*Involves climbing about
1000 feet twice.*

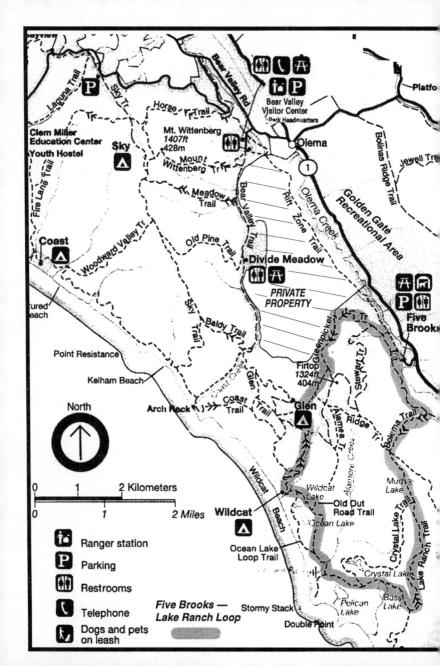

O n a bright Sunday morning in early spring I took off up the Stewart Trail out of the Five Brooks Trailhead at a good clip. Moving through the deep forest of Douglas fir for a mile and a half, I came upon the junction of the Stewart Trail and the Greenpicker Trail. Both trails lead up to the Ridge Trail slightly over 1000 vertical feet above Five Brooks. The climb to the Ridge Trail is about 2.8 miles by either trail from Five Brooks. Figure three miles via the Stewart Trail and 2.8 miles by branching off the Stewart Trail and taking the Greenpicker Trail[1]. Both trails climb up somewhat steeply through the deep forest. On this particular morning I chose to take the Greenpicker Trail. The Greenpicker Trail is narrower than the Stewart Trail. It appears to have been a ranch road many years ago for it is much overgrown, whereas the Stewart Trail is still used by the Park Service for vehicular patrol out to Wildcat Camp.

On the Greenpicker Trail I observed two delightful picnic spots, both to the left of the trail and at the base of short steep rises. I came upon the first a short distance from the Greenpicker-Stewart junction, a gently sloping and small green meadow partly shaded by large Douglas firs and bay trees to the left of the trail at the base of the first abrupt climb (50 yards up 100-150 vertical feet). The second picnic spot came 10-15 minutes of steady hiking later. It was 40 feet to the left of a slightly longer and steeper rise at 1000 feet above sea level on the topographical map. The second spot, like the first, was small, intimate, and partly shaded by large Douglas firs. The old Greenpicker Trail gradually leveled off, dipped up and down, and then swung into more open and level terrain.

---

[1] Actually the Greenpicker Trail now turns west to Glen Camp at a point some 300 to 400 yards from the open meadow at Fir Top. However, the old Greenpicker Trail continues, from this junction, along the wooded ridge to Fir Top and is clearly discernable. Meanwhile, the revised (1983) Greenpicker Trail plunges through a deep conifer forest for about 1.5 miles to Glen Camp.

The old Greenpicker Trail turned southward along the wooded Inverness Ridge, for a short distance, until it turned sharply westward and downward at a point marked with a trail sign. I continued straight ahead on the wooded ridge for a few hundred yards before coming upon the broad open meadow know as Fir Top. At Fir Top the trail junctioned with the Stewart Trail coming up from Five Brooks to the east.

On this particular bright spring morning, with the warm air bringing out the sweet scent of pine, I followed the Stewart Trail which drops away immediately to the south of Fir Top.

Within a few hundred yards of my having departed from Fir Top on the Stewart Trail, I came upon its junction with the Ridge Trail coming in from left (southeast). The Ridge Trail crosses the Stewart Trail and continues northwestward for a short distance steps before junctioning with the Greenpicker Trail. The Stewart Trail continued a southward course for one mile, dropping 400 vertical feet in that distance. The trail then veered temporarily northwestward for 1/2 mile to a junction with the Glen Trail. At the junction the trail signs clearly pointed out the options. A right turn on the Glen Trail would have taken me 1.2 miles uphill to Glen Camp. But, headed for the sea, I turned left and southwest towards Wildcat Camp 1.2 miles away.

As I dropped westward on the Stewart Trail I became aware of a rising wind as the forest began giving way to open brush country. The air was clear, crisp, and cool. Occasionally I caught a glimpse of Drakes Bay and the Pacific Ocean. In .5 mile I came upon the junction of the Stewart Trail and the Coast Trail coming up from Wildcat Beach and joining the Stewart Trail in a northward turn towards Bear Valley. I continued straight ahead and downhill on the

Coast Trail also the Stewart Trail towards Wildcat Camp .7 mile ahead.

In five minutes I broke out into full view of the broad green meadow which marks Wildcat Camp some 400 feet below the trail. 500 yards of additional descent brought me out onto the sunlit meadow where the grass was sparkling in the noon sun and dancing in a sharp wind out of the northwest.

After a short lunch in a sheltered spot on the beach nearby I resumed my hike on the Coast Trail as it climbs steeply to the east for about 150 yards before turning southward. About 200 yards from Wildcat Camp the Coast Trail meets the Ocean-Lake Loop Trail which veers off to the right, passing to the west of Wildcat Lake 300 yards from the junction. The Ocean Lake Loop Trail continues in open country and offers a fine view of the sea. In about 1/2 mile Ocean-Lake is reached. Passing onward (southward) one comes upon a small footpath branching off the Ocean-Lake Loop Trail and descending along a small cascade to the beach immediately north of Alamere Falls (a good way to reach the falls for a side trip). This footpath is but a few yards from Ocean-Lake.

On this day I chose to move along the winding and open Coast Trail past Wildcat Lake towards beautiful Pelican Lake (two miles from Wildcat Camp and off the trail) to the southern junction with the Ocean-Lake Loop Trail. Some 500 yards beyond the southern junction with the Ocean-Lake Loop Trail the Coast Trail crosses Alamere Creek, climbs up some 130 vertical feet over some 250 to 300 yards, and connects with a small footpath, somewhat overgrown, which circumvents much of the western overgrown shore of Pelican Lake. From the junction with the footpath, Coast Trail climbs gradually for about 150 feet over 700 yards. Then the trail begins to level off and turn away from Pelican Lake below. At this point one can take a short diversion to discover a magnificent panorama of Pelican Lake, much of the Drakes Bay coastline and Point Reyes. Follow an overgrown footpath through coyote brush for 250 to 300 yards to an open hill south of your departure point on the Coast Trail. From the hill one of the finest and most unique views in Point Reyes National Seashore can be enjoyed. But watch out for poison oak along the first 50-60 yards of the footpath.

Back on the Coast Trail, I found myself moving into the forest, for some 500 yards, to the north shore of Bass Lake.[2] Here picnickers had launched a plastic raft and were busily paddling across the lake. Pelican and Bass Lakes are about 3/4 mile in circumference each. Wildcat and Ocean Lakes are about 1/2 mile in circumference, but marshy. Crystal Lake is 1/2 mile northeast of Pelican Lake and can be reached by a small trail branching off to the left of the Coast Trail about half way between Pelican and Bass Lakes.

3/4 mile beyond Bass Lake, I found myself at the junction of the Coast Trail and the Lake Ranch Trail. Near the junction, at a point where nine large fir trees are to be seen to the right or west of the Coast Trail, the old Lake Ranch homestead stood.

The Lake Ranch Trail climbs for 650' over three miles. I found an increasingly fine view as I climbed through open terrain, the brush covered western slope of the Inverness Ridge. White and purple bush lupines brightened the steady climb which, in two miles from the junction with the Coast Trail, began leading into the deep forest

[2]Bass Lake is a 12 acre springfed lake approximately 150 feet deep. Although you won't find bass, you can anticipate seeing such wild life as ducks and deer. The water temperature of around 58 to 60 degrees makes it appealing for swimming. No camping is allowed.

of the Inverness Ridge. By the time I was 1/2 mile from Mud Lake I was well into the forest with Drakes Bay entirely hidden by towering and thick Douglas fir.

A half mile beyond Mud Lake and in gently rolling but generally level terrain, I came to the junction of the Lake Ranch Trail, Ridge Trail, and Bolema Trail. With the sun already dropping on the western horizon, I took the shorter route back to Five Brooks by way of the Bolema Trail, and, after one mile, the Olema Valley Trail, a total distance of 2-3 miles from the 3-way trail junction[3]. My route, mostly wooded, was marked by forget-me-nots, just beginning to come up along the edge of the trail. The road trail "switched-back" its way down the eastern slope of the Inverness Ridge, and at a few points I discovered a fine view up the Olema Valley, through which runs the rift zone of the San Andreas Earthquake fault, and of portions of the ridges on either side of the valley. In contrast to this wooded eastern slope of the rift zone-Olema Valley, the western slope (culminating in the Bolinas Ridge) is open and generally unwooded in its lower portion.

I came upon the small pond at the Five Brooks Trailhead as the sinking sun cast long shadows across the meadows. How I never tire of this magnificent land.

---

[3] 2.3 miles from the Coast Trail the Lake Ranch Trail junctions with the Crystal Lake Trail coming up from Crystal Lake 3.3 miles to the west. A beautiful route!

On the Ridge Trail.

The Palomarin – Lake Ranch – Ridge Trails Loop

- *Palomarin Trailhead • Lake Ranch site*
- *Lake Ranch Trail • Mud Lake*
- *Ridge Trail/Bolema Trail/Lake Ranch Trail junction*
- *Ridge Trail • Mesa Road • Palomarin Trailhead*

---

10 – 11 miles
- *Involves 1100 vertical feet of climbing and descending.*
Moderate

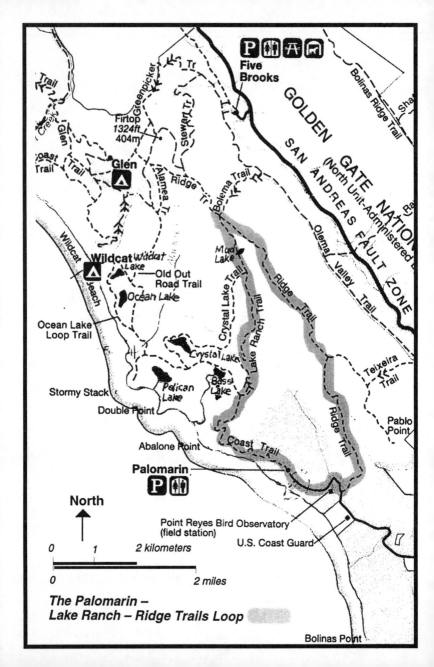

North

0   1   2 kilometers

0   2 miles

The Palomarin –
Lake Ranch – Ridge Trails Loop

W e started up on a calm spring morning, as a fog was lifting, from Palomarin Trailhead. Starting out on the Coast Trail we were soon winding along an open coastal shelf. Wild mustard, ice plant, golden poppies, iris, buttercups, cowsnips, monkey flower, wild rose, lupines, morning glory, daffodils, and poison oak all made themselves evident as the bright sunlight burned away the last traces of fog. A northwest wind, typical for spring afternoons, began to set the tall grass to dancing. In less than a mile the trail turned away from the coast and gradually took up northerly and upward directions to the junction with the Lake Ranch Trail. We considered going on along the Coast Trail to one of the lakes — Bass, Crystal, or Pelican — for lunch, something which can be easily worked in with this particular hike, but such a diversion would have lengthened our hike by two or three miles and we had started late from Palomarin.

Going up the Lake Ranch Trail, we found the sides of the trail alive with all the wildflowers previously mentioned plus Indian paint brush and thistle. Sage and manzanita began to make their appearance. The air, which had been quite cool right along the Coast Trail from Palomarin to the junction with the Lake Ranch Trail, was now warmer, having been heated by the inland hills through which we were now passing.

In the 1/2 mile beyond Mud Lake the Lake Ranch Trail meets the Bolema Trail and the Ridge Trail in the deep fir forest. We turned southeast and started out on the Ridge Trail.

The Ridge Trail had been winding for slightly over 1 1/2 miles southeastward from its northern terminus at "Fir Top" when it reached this junction with the Bolema and Lake Ranch Trails. Throughout these 1.5 miles the trail is shaded by giant Douglas firs and fringed, occasionally, by tiny patches of green meadow, ferns, and huckleberry. From the junction on towards Palomarin, the southern terminus of the trail, the Ridge Trail continues to be shaded by the abundant firs. However, I soon came upon evidence of indiscriminate logging — probably from an earlier time by 10 or 15 years. Numerous stumps between 10 and 24 inches in diameter were scattered amid coyote brush and manzanita. A few mature firs remained, but the young firs, 10 to 20 feet in height, were more numerous.

The Ridge Trail rolled gently up and down. The fluctuations in altitude were never more than 50 to 100 feet and were always gradual. Occasionally we came upon fine views of the Bolinas Ridge across the Olema Valley to the east. But to the west, the ocean was effectively blocked from view by the forest because most of the timber cutting had taken place on the east side of the Ridge Trail. California lilac bushes were in bloom in the areas where the cutting had been more widespread as were blackberry vines. 2.5 miles from the Bolema — Lake Ranch — Ridge trails junction we came upon another junction. Breaking off to the left is a trail, which is .7 miles, comes upon still another junction. Here a left turn takes one on the Teixeria Trail and a right turn to Pablo Point a mile from the second junction. The wooded Teixeria Trail drops steeply in its .5 mile length. It connects with Olema Valley Trail and the McCurdy Trail leading east and out of Point Reyes National Seashore to the Bolinas Ridge. In just under 5 miles the Olema Valley Trail which closely parallels the San Andreas earthquake fault line, comes into Five Brooks Trailhead just off of Francis Drake Blvd. If one continues from Five Brooks on the Rift Zone Trail the Bear Valley Trailhead (Visitor Center) is reached in 4.3 miles of hiking alternately through wooded glens and open meadows. From the aforementioned junction the one mile trail to Pablo Point passes through deep woods, occasional sections of bush, and reaches the open meadows around Pablo Point from where, in places, there is a fine view of the Bolinas Mesa, the Bolinsa Lagoon, and the Sunset district of San Francisco.

We kept on the Ridge Trail which began immediately to drop. In about a 1/2 mile from the junction we broke out onto a high and open hill commanding a magnificent view of Bolinas Lagoon, Stinson Beach, the Bolinas Ridge, the western shoulder of Mount Tamalpais, and San Francisco west of Twin Peaks. The land mass around Sharp Park and Pacifica jetted prominently into the sea and could easily have been mistaken for an island by someone who was ignorant of the San Francisco Bay Area's geography.

The remainder of the route along the Ridge Trail involved a steady drop southward for 100-150 yards then an abrupt westward turn over open hills just coming alive with wildflowers — bluegrass, lupines, Indian paint brush, and iris. In one mile from the scenic picnic spot just behind us the trail dropped about 600-700 vertical feet to Mesa Road, the roadway which connects Bolinas to the Palomarin Trailhead. Once on Mesa Road we had a 1.2 mile winding trek which we covered very quickly in order to avoid the exposure to dust stirred up by autos on the Mesa Road.

On the last mile along Mesa Road we passed the Point Reyes Bird Observatory, which is dedicated to the preservation of bird life within the National Seashore area. At the observatory are situated both a small museum and a bird watchers' lookout.

Moving on, we came to the Palomarin parking lot as both the nearby grass and distant sea danced wildly in the typical springtime wind.

Dairy cattle at the mouth of Abbotts Lagoon.

The Point Reyes Beach Hike

- *Point Reyes Beach South*
- *Point Reyes Beach North*
- *Abbotts Lagoon* • *Kehoe Beach*
- *Return To Point Reyes.*

14 – 15 miles*
Moderate
- *Level hiking on beach sand*

*Leave a pick-up car at Abbotts Lagoon area and cut this hike by 7+ miles.

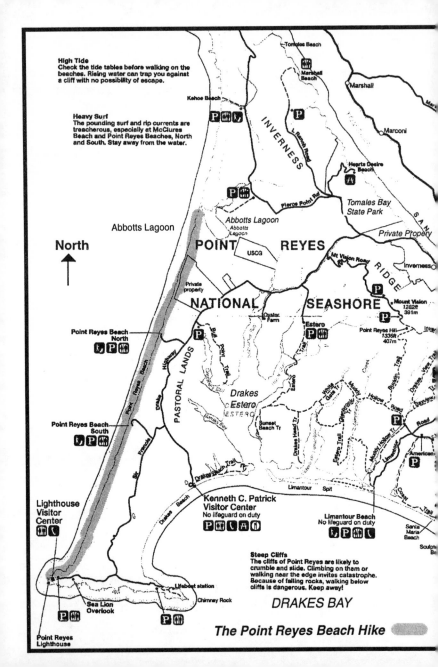

High Tide
Check the tide tables before walking on the beaches. Rising water can trap you against a cliff with no possibility of escape.

Heavy Surf
The pounding surf and rip currents are treacherous, especially at McClures Beach and Point Reyes Beaches, North and South. Stay away from the water.

Kehoe Beach

INVERNESS

Marshall Beach

Tomales Beach

Marshall

Marconi

Hearts Desire Beach

Tomales Bay State Park

Private Property

Pierce Point Rd

Abbotts Lagoon

Abbotts Lagoon

North

POINT   **REYES**

USCG

Mt Vision Road

Inverness

Private property

NATIONAL   **SEASHORE**

Mount Vision
1282ft
391m

Oyster Farm

Estero

Point Reyes Hill
1336ft
407m

Point Reyes Beach North

Bull Point Trail

Estero

White Gate Tr

Muddy Hollow

Bucksin Trail

Drakes View Tr

Bayview Tr

Point Reyes Highway

Drakes Estero
ESTERO

Sunset Beach Tr

Drakes Head Tr

Glenbrook

Estero Trail

Muddy Hollow Tr

Bayview Road

Point Reyes Beach South

Francis

Limantour Rd

American

Coast Trail

Drakes Beach Trail

Sir

Lighthouse Visitor Center

Drakes Beach

Kenneth C. Patrick Visitor Center
No lifeguard on duty

Limantour Spit

Limantour Beach
No lifeguard on duty

Santa Maria Beach

Sculptured Beach

Steep Cliffs
The cliffs of Point Reyes are likely to crumble and slide. Climbing on them or walking near the edge invites catastrophe. Because of falling rocks, walking below cliffs is dangerous. Keep away!

Sea Lion Overlook

Lifeboat station

Chimney Rock

DRAKES BAY

Point Reyes Lighthouse

The Point Reyes Beach Hike

G oing up Point Reyes Beach from the point itself to McClures Beach is a unique experience. We hiked from the sandy beach just north and down a sandy hill from the Sir Francis Drake Highway as it comes to within 500 yards of the Point Reyes Lighthouse. Our descent to the beach, 400-450 vertical feet below, took us down a gentle and sandy slope. The route was strictly cross country so one should use a topographical map and do a little reconoitering to find the easiest way down to the beach.

Once on the beach, we turned northward and began a long and somewhat monotonous sandy hike towards Abbotts Lagoon. Varied configurations of driftwood were scattered all along the beach some 100 to 150 feet back from the water. Many of the pieces were huge logs which may have originated in any one of the many large rivers of northern California and Oregon, only to be cast up by heavy storms. Behind the driftwood a low ridge of dunes stretched endlessly northwards towards McClures Beach, vaguely visible on the northern horizon. The dunes stretched inland for a few hundred yards. Clumps of dune grass protruded up through the fine granules of white sand. It was too early in the year for yellow lupines, but in spring a few clumps may be found farther inland between the first ridge of dunes and the Sir Francis Drake Highway.

2.5 miles up the beach we came upon what is now Point Reyes Beach South, a stretch of beach accessible by auto since the Park Service has built a road less than a mile in length linking Sir Francis Drake Highway with Point Reyes Beach. Point Reyes Beach South is not distinct from the beach anywhere on this long expanse of ocean front. In fact, the only truly distinctive landmark along the entire route from Point Reyes itself to McClures Beach is Abbotts Lagoon, 8.5 miles from where we started our great sand trek.

In another two miles we came upon the beach now known as Point Reyes Beach North. Today the National Park Service maintains a beach access facility — parking lot, rest rooms, bulletin board, garbage cans, and ranger patrol.

I was taken with the steep angle with which the beach dropped off into the sea and with the power of the breakers on what was a windless day. The surf was in constant turmoil. The roar of crashing breakers, punctuated by the high pitched swish of seawater churning onto the sand close to our feet, was constant.

7-8 miles from our starting point at the northern base of the northern cliffs of Point Reyes itself we came upon Abbotts Lagoon. The Lagoon is 4-5 miles in circumference. Its brackish water serves as a stop over spot for migrating birds. The Lagoon[1] is surrounded by broad dunes that suggest an ancient inlet or bay for the eastern end of the lagoon is over a mile inland from the sea. We had wondered if the lagoon was connected with the sea, but found that a low sandbar separated the two. A storm, however, could easily pour ocean water over the sandbar and into the lagoon.

On the return hike from Abbotts Lagoon to Point Reyes we loitered to examine the driftwood, eat dinner, and take a few pictures. Miles before reaching Point Reyes and our sandy hill climb to the autos, we were overtaken by darkness. The night was moonless but a million stars glittered overhead to give just enough light to enable us to see our way down the beach. We couldn't see the breakers, but we could hear them pounding constantly. The lighthouse at Point

[1] The Lagoon is immediately accessible from the Pierce Point Road, off of which the National Park Service maintains a small trailhead. One can leave a pick-up car here to cut this hike in half.

Reyes was not visible, nor was there any man-made light to be seen anywhere. The night air was still and the monotony of crashing breakers was broken only by the occasional screech of an unseen seagull. The faint silhouette of Point Reyes gradually became more and more distinct indicating that we were making

Point Reyes Beach — view from Kehoe Beach to Point Reyes.

progress towards our destination. For over two hours we hiked in almost total darkness except for the starlight above.

We reached the base of our sandy hill unexpectedly because we could not see it until we were actually on it. There were two flashlights in a party of 15, and we had purposely saved them for this last part of the hike. With their help we struggled up the sandy hill to our autos, waiting in the darkness at the Lighthouse parking lot at the terminus of the Sir Francis Drake Highway. Far out to sea a ship light flashed periodically as we took a last look at the black mass of land and sea. And from somewhere in that vast and dark mass we could hear, more distant now but as incessant as ever, the eternal crash of breakers on Point Reyes Beach.

On Kelham Beach.

Other Hikes in
Point Reyes National Seashore

• *Palomarin Trailhead to Bear Valley Trailhead (13.9 miles)* • *Five Brooks Trailhead to Bear Valley Trailhead (11.8 miles)* • *Limantour Beach to Palomarin Trailhead (15.1 miles)* • *Bear Valley Trailhead to Limantour Beach (8.5 miles)*
• *Bayview-Muddy Hollow (5.0 miles)* • *Rift Zone Trail (4.4 miles)* • *Earthquake Trail (.7 mile)*

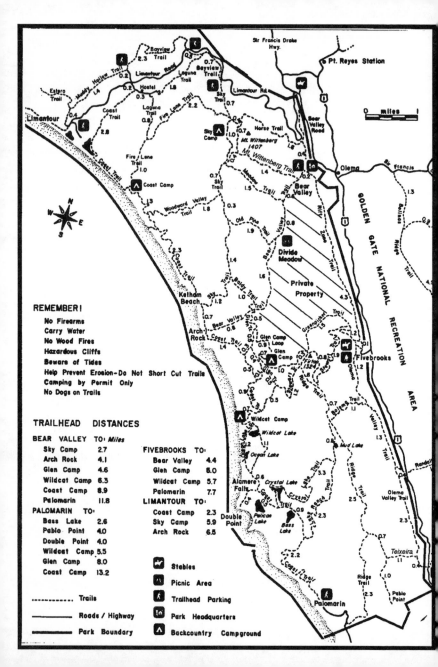

PALOMARIN TRAILHEAD to
BEAR VALLEY TRAILHEAD

This hike can be taken in reverse. It's just as beautiful one way as the other. Arbitrarily, I'll start you at Palomarin. Proceed on the Coast Trail to the Lake Ranch Trail junction (2.2 miles), continue on the Coast Trail past Bass Lake, Pelican Lake, Ocean Lake, and Wildcat Lake to Wildcat camp (5.4 miles from Palomarin). From Wildcat Camp go up the Coast Trail to Arch Rock (8.5 miles from Palomarin Trailhead). From Arch Rock pick up the Bear Valley Trail and hike on to Bear Valley Trailhead 4.4 miles from Miller Point. Total distance 13.9 miles.

   • *Moderate.* • *About 1200 feet of climbing and descending.*

FIVE BROOKS TRAILHEAD to
BEAR VALLEY TRAILHEAD

Start at Five Brooks and go up the Stewart Trail or Stewart and Greenpicker Trails to Fir Top (3 miles from Five Brooks via Stewart Trail). Proceed west on Stewart Trail to the junction with the Glen Trail (5.2 miles from Five Brooks). Continue down the Stewart Trail to its junction with the Coast Trail (5.8 miles from Five Brooks via Stewart Trail). Go up the Coast Trail to its junction with the small unnamed trail connecting it with the Glen Trail (north end) about 1.7 miles from Wildcat Camp. On the Glen Trail, continue first level, then downhill and northward to the junction with the Bear Valley Trail (8.6 miles from Five Brooks). Proceed to Bear Valley Trailhead (3.2 miles). Total distance 11.8 miles.

   • *Moderate.* • *A shorter route between these two trailheads (9 miles) can be put together.*

LIMANTOUR BEACH (or Point Reyes Hostel) to PALOMARIN TRAILHEAD

Proceed on Coast Trail to Coast Camp (3 miles from Point Reyes Hostel). Continue south on Coast Trail to junction with Woodward Valley Trail (4.3 miles from the Hostel). Continue south to the Kellum Beach (6.5 miles from the Hostel) and to Arch Rock overlook (7.3 miles from the Hostel). Climb up on the Coast Trail to its connection with the Glen Trail (1.4 miles from Miller Point) and follow the Coast Trail down to Wildcat Beach (3 miles from Arch Rock). From Wildcat Beach take the Coast Trail southward on past Wildcat Lake, Pelican Lake, and Bass Lake to the junction with the Lake Ranch Trail (13 miles from the Hostel). Continue on the Coast Trail to Palomarin two miles ahead. Total distance 15 miles.

> • *Moderate-strenuous. About 1000 feet of up and down hill hiking is involved.*

BEAR VALLEY TRAILHEAD to the POINT REYES HOSTEL (or Limantour Beach)

Proceed down the Bear Valley Trail to the junction with Mt. Wittenberg Trail (200-250 yards from Bear Valley Trailhead). Go up the Mt. Wittenberg Trail to Mount Wittenberg (1.8 miles from Bear Valley Trailhead). Drop down to the Sky Trail from Mount Wittenberg (.2 miles). Follow the Sky Trail to its junction with the Fire Lane (3 miles from Bear Valley Trailhead). Follow the Fire Lane (described in detail in Chapter 4) down to Coast Camp and the Coast Trail. Proceed along the Coast Trail to the Hostel (8.5 miles from Bear Valley Trailhead). Total distance 8.5 miles. For a more direct route to the Hostel take the Laguna Trail off the Fire Lane (2.2 miles from the junction of the Fire Lane and Sky Trail) and follow it (.8 mile) to the Hostel.

- *Easy except for a 1200' climb to top of Mount Wittenberg.*

BAYVIEW — MUDDY HOLLOW HIKE

Have someone who is heading down the Limantour Road to Limantour Beach (the Park Service maintains the road and a parking lot near the beach) drop you off at the Bayview Trailhead at the crest of the Limantour Road where it crosses the Olema Ridge. The Bayview Trail is well surrounded, at its outset, by the unique Bishop pine, lilac bushes, and coyote brush.

After about a mile of gentle down hill walking one breaks out into semi-open hills with the first view of Drakes Bay. From then on the trail drops more sleeply over increasingly open hills to the Muddy Hollow Trailhead about 3 miles from the Bayview Trailhead. The Muddy Hollow Trail is a naturalist's delight as it moves along a generally straight and level course to the sea 1.75 miles from the Trailhead. In evidence are groves of alders, blackberry bushes, Queen Anne's lace, cowslips, blue grass, Indian paint brush, cattails, blue lupine, yellow monkey flower, orange monkey flower and wild oats. From Muddy Hollow, just behind the dunes of Limantour Beach, one can go on a few hundred yards to the Limantour parking lot to meet his or her ride.

- *A pleasant down hill 5 mile saunter with plant and animal life to enjoy.*

THE RIFT ZONE TRAIL

The Rift Zone Trail connects Five Brooks Trailhead with the Bear Valley Trailhead at Olema. The trail moves through level terrain and is generally parallel to the San Andreas Earthquake faultline. A sophisticated viewer can see evidence of the faultline while hiking from Five Brooks Trailhead to the Bear Valley Trailhead. In fact, the Rift Zone Trail crosses the earthquake fault some 200 yards south of the Bear Valley Trailhead parking lot.

The Rift Zone Trail, which crosses the private Vedanta Religious Retreat, passes through green meadows (expect to see cattle grazing in the first mile south of Bear Valley Trailhead), through forests of fir, madrone, oak, and alder, and emerges once again into open meadows. This is a gentle hike and one which is especially suited for families with small children. Transportation is the only problem, since one starts at one trailhead and finishes at another. Explore having someone pick you up. This is particularly desirable if one is making this hike with small children.

For anyone, this is a beautifully pastoral region which should be hiked very leisurely to be enjoyed.

- *Total distance 4.4 miles. Easy.*

THE EARTHQUAKE TRAIL

An exciting feature of Point Reyes National Seashore is the presence of the San Andreas earthquake faultline. The earthquake faultline comes into Marin County and the National Seashore from under the Pacific Ocean off the mouth of Tomales Bay. It runs under Tomales Bay, then overland through the Park Headquarters at Olema, and down the Olema Valley to the sea just off Stinson Beach.

The linear Tomales Bay gives clear indication of the direction of the faultline. At the Park Headquarters there are cypress trees, just opposite (northward) the Administration Building, which were displaced by the 1906 earthquake. The faultline runs smack under the road from which you will be turning into the Visitor Center.

Just past the Visitor Center and Headquarters is the parking area known as Bear Valley Trailhead. The Earthquake Trail, a .7 mile loop walk which is a kind of self-guided tour of various points of geologic and historic interest along the fault line, begins at the southeast edge of the unpaved parking area diagonally across from the Visitor Center. The trail begins in front of a wooden restroom facility. Don't miss an old fence, which was displaced some 18 feet in 1906 by the lateral shifting of the earth's surface. Still standing today, it is a testimonial to the colossal power of earthquakes.

At the location of the displaced fence, one can look towards the red barn and see a line of blue stakes which have been positioned to mark the actual faultline.

  • *A .7 mile walk. Wheelchair accessible.*

PHILLIP BURTON WILDERNESS AREA & RESEARCH NATURAL AREA

A true Wilderness area you might consider exploring if you wish to get away from shared trails. There is minimum impact or human interference. No mountain bikes are allowed. The area is clearly marked on the park brochure.

A FINAL NOTE

In this trail guide I have attempted to describe the major trails and points of natural and aesthetic interest in Point Reyes National

Seashore. Any of these can be modified to suit the interest of the particular hiker.

I have not suggested all of the hikes that one can take in Point Reyes National Seashore. For me to list every possible hike would be to take much of the joy and adventure out of letting one put one's own hike plan together. So the hiker who wishes to put together his or her own particular hike plan can use this guide plus any combination of maps to do just that.

Safety Alerts

• *ticks* • *poison oak* • *stinging nettle*
• *beaches* • *mountain lions* • *water*

TICKS

Ticks that carry Lyme disease are known to occur in Point Reyes National Seashore. Stay on trails and check your clothing frequently. The quicker ticks are removed and the area washed, the less the chance of transmittal of the organism that causes illness. Wearing light colored, long pants helps you spot them and tucking the bottom of your pants inside your socks helps keep the ticks from crawling up your legs. Always check your body completely at the end of your hike.

POISON OAK

Poison oak has three smooth shiny leaflets and is usually bright green but often has a red coloration in new shoots and in dry the season. There is lots of poison oak in the Point Reyes National Seashore area, particularly in forested regions. If hiking on established and maintained trails, there is less danger of coming in contact with poison oak, however. If going off-trail, other than along the beach, wear long trousers and a long-sleeved shirt. Thoroughly wash any skin that may have come in contact with the plant with cool water and a grease cutting dish soap. Be sure to also wash all clothing before wearing again. *Tecnu,* available in most drug stores, is the best known substance to wash poison oak oil off the skin, but don't use Tecnu on the trail. It is effective up to 12 hours after contact. Poison oak is systemic, which means you may break out in body locations other than the initial point of contact.

STINGING NETTLE

Stinging nettle is a tall weedy plant with needlelike projections which inject a chemical into your skin, creating a burning sensation for up to 24 hours.

If you are unsure what this plant looks like, stop by at a visitor center before starting your hike.

BEACHES

The National Seashore offers a diversity of beaches to explore. However, if you plan to spend any time near the shoreline stay aware of the movement of the tides. Consult a tide book before going tidepooling. Always keep an eye on the surf and watch for occasional, especially large waves, called sneaker waves. Also remember, since fire permits are issued for beach fires, hot coals may exist below the surface if fires have not been extinguished properly. Wearing shoes on beaches is recommended.

MOUNTAIN LIONS

Mountain lions do live in the park and your paths may cross. Sighting a majestic lion is a rare treat. Generally, there is no need to fear lions. However *if you should encounter a lion, follow these guidelines:*

- If you have little children, do not allow them to hike or walk ahead of you. If you encounter a lion, pick small children up.

Keyhole at northern end of Secret Beach.

- Do not run. Mountain lions associate running with prey and may chase you. Hold your ground, or move slowly away while facing the lion.

- Do not crouch down; try to appear as large as possible.

- If the lion behaves aggressively, wave your hands, shout, and throw sticks, packs, etc. at it. This action protects you and "teaches" the lion that humans are not good prey.

WATER

Public health authorities have determined that it is unsafe to drink the water in the Point Reyes National Seashore area. It is especially advisable to avoid the water in summer and fall during a very dry year, and never to drink the water from lakes, or stream water which is not moving rapidly. Always carry liquids with you.

IF YOU GET LOST WHILE HIKING

Marked trails are those whose starting point and junctions with other trails are marked with a trail sign which at least tells the hiker the name of the trail he or she is about to follow. The markers usually include, also, an indication of the distance to the next junction and/or location. If you should get lost, or firmly believe you are lost, head for any Trailhead: Bear Valley, Palomarin, Five Brooks, Limantour, Estero Trail, Muddy Hollow, McClures, Tomales Point, Bayview. At any of these trailheads you will find a parking lot and, most likely, other hikers and automobiles. At the Bear Valley Trailhead you will find permanent ranger headquarters and a public phone (should you arrive after the Visitor Center closes at 5 p.m.).

If by some *remote* chance you get lost and are caught by darkness without flashlight, stay where you are until first light. Dress warmly, stay under trees and away from the open meadows or beach where it will be colder. The only thing which can hurt you under such circumstances is panic. Exposure is not a problem for anyone stuck overnight so long as one stays calm, dry and out of any wind.

A raincoat or pancho should be taken if there is the slightest possibility of a rainstorm. Even on warm days, because the temperature can change, one should always carry a heavy sweater or parka in a knapsack. If you are forced to spend the night, *do not start a fire*. It could easily get away from you and greatly complicate matters. Stay among the trees and try to sleep. When you walk out the next morning, tell a ranger you're out and okay just in case it's your friends and/or family who panicked. The main thing is — you didn't!

Coast Miwok Indian Village.

Places of Interest
In and Around
Point Reyes National Seashore

- *Coast Miwok Indian Village*
- *Morgan Horse Ranch*
- *Point Reyes Lighthouse* •*Beaches*
- *Tomales Bay State Park* •*Point Reyes Bird Observatory* • *Audubon Canyon Ranch*
- *Gulf of the Farallones National Marine Sanctuary*
- *Lifeboat Station* • *Hog & Duck Island*

COAST MIWOK INDIAN VILLAGE &
CULTURAL EXHIBIT

This replica of a Coast Miwok Indian Village, at Point Reyes National Seashore gives us an idea of the way of life of these Native Americans who lived here for thousands of years before the arrival of Europeans.

The Coast Miwoks lived as hunters and gatherers in Marin and southern Sonoma counties in village communities we call triblets. It is estimated the Coast Miwok Indians inhabited over 100 such villages on the Point Reyes peninsula at the time of Sir Francis Drake's supposed visit in 1579.

Open daily sunrise to sunset. Staffed between 9:30 a.m. and 3:30 p.m. on weekends, at which time additional artifacts may be viewed.

On the first Saturday of every month, you may take part in the ongoing tasks of maintaining the structures and area.

Festivals are offered three times each year. Inquire at the Visitor Center for information regarding dates.

The village was built by volunteers under the direction of the National Park Service and the Miwok Archeological Preserve of Marin.

For additional information, refer to **Kule Loklo** and the **Coast Miwok Indians,** published by Coastal Parks Association and Miwok Archeological Preserve of Marin(1982), and **The Coast Miwok Indians of the Point Reyes Area**, published by the Point Reyes National Seashore Association(1993). Available for sale at the Visitor Center.

MORGAN HORSE RANCH

A special attraction at Point Reyes National Seashore is the **Morgan Horse Ranch**, located just off the upper parking lot near the Bear Valley Headquarters.

The working horse ranch is one of the locations in the National Park Service where horses are trained for use by Park Rangers. Exhibits, corrals, demonstrations are all part of the ongoing interpretive program of the ranch.

- *Open seven days a week*
- *9 am to 4:30 pm*
- *telephone: (415) 663-1763*

POINT REYES LIGHTHOUSE

The Lighthouse is operated under the auspices of the National Park Service as an Historic Site.

- *Open 10:00 a.m. to 4:30 p.m.*
- *Closed Tuesday and Wednesday.*

Over 300 steps lead down the cliff to the Lighthouse. The windswept observation area affords incredible views.

The Lighthouse sits 265 feet above the ocean. Constructed in 1870, it houses the French-built Fresnel lens. The beam is 294 feet above sea level.

March, April and May and November, December and January are the best months for visiting, since there is generally heavy fog during the summer months. Whether you visit for wildflower viewing in May, or whale watching in the winter months, Point Reyes Lighthouse will not disappoint you. The Lighthouse and its environs afford the best vantage point for whale watching at the National Seashore because the point extends so far west into the open sea.

Dress warmly, as it will probably be windy and or foggy. Up to 2700 hours of fog have been recorded yearly.

Evening Lighthouse tour. Dress warmly and bring a flashlight for a dusk lighting of the giant crystal lens. Limited space available on this popular program. Call (415) 669-1534 after 10:00 am the day of the tour for reservations. 1 hour.

For more information, call (415) 663-1092 or (415) 699-1534.

BEACHES ACCESSIBLE TO AUTOMOBILES

There are eight beaches in Point Reyes National Seashore which are accessible from the road. For specific road directions, consult your California State Highway map. Five of the beaches — **Point Reyes Beach South, Point Reyes Beach North, Abbotts Lagoon and Beach, Kehoe Beach** and **McClures Beach** — are situated on the open sea and are excellent for sunbathing, picnicking and general enjoyment. However, they are all characterized by strong undertow and treacherous rip tides. **Do not go in the water. Drakes Beach** and **Limantour Beach** are also good for picnicking, sunbathing, sand castling and relaxing.

These two beaches, being situated on Drakes Bay, are considered suitable for wading and swimming. **Marshall Beach** is situated on Tomales Bay where waters are generally calmer, and the beach is more sheltered from the winds. There are no lifeguards anywhere at Drakes or Limantour Beaches, however, and one swims at his or her own risk.

Please remember, it is against the law to remove living organisms from tidepools.

*   *   *

LIMANTOUR BEACH is perhaps the most popular beach because of its relatively broad beach and dunes. Along with Drakes Beach and Marshall Beach, it is less windy than the other beaches. The access road, which extends some 8.9 miles from the Bear Valley Trailhead to the Limantour parking lot, was severly damaged by the flood of 1982 and is now open.

DRAKES BEACH on Drakes Bay is 15.3 miles from the Bear Valley Trailhead or Olema. You can drive right to the beach, where you will find a spacious parking area, restrooms, picnic tables and a beach house, book store and snackbar. The broad, flat sandy beach is sheltered and excellent for picnicking. Fires are allowed on the beach. There is swimming and, on good days, surfers can be seen riding the breakers. The alleged site of Sir Francis Drake's landing is located 1.5 miles down (southeast) the beach and just inside Drakes Estero. A small plaque commemorates the point where Drake may have careened his *Golden Hinde* vessel in June 1579 for repairs. In addition, a granite cross monument to Drake's landing is adjacent to the parking lot. **The Ken Patrick Visitor Center** at Drakes Beach has been expanded to provide additional space for viewing and exhibitry focusing on 16th century exploration and the marine environment. A salt water aquarium is home to plant and animal life from the bay. A minke whale skeleton is also on display, and you can also experience an eel's eye view of life beyond the surf. Rangers are on hand to answer your questions. Open weekends and holidays 10:00 am to 5:00 pm. Closed for lunch noon-12:30 pm. Telephone: (415) 699-1250.

ABBOTTS LAGOON AND BEACH is eleven miles by road from the Bear Valley Trailhead or Olema. A small parking area, with restroom facilities, can accommodate some ten to twelve automobiles. An easy 1 1/4 mile walk over level terrain takes you from the parking area to Abbotts Lagoon, some magnificent dunes, and the open sea. Sunbathing and wading are usually best along the mouth of the lagoon. Canoeing and kayaking are permitted on the Lagoon, which is a migratory bird habitat.

KEHOE BEACH, 2.2 miles past the Abbotts Lagoon parking area, is 13.2 miles from the Bear Valley Trailhead. The only parking area is along the shoulder of the road. A 3/4 mile level walk leads to the beach, which offers miles of dunes to choose from in order to picnic or find shelter on windy days. A stile at the road marks the unmaintained trail to the beach. There is a roadside restroom.

McCLURES BEACH is 3.7 miles from Kehoe Beach and 16.9 miles from the Bear Valley Trailhead. A twisty and steep 1/2 mile downhill trail down a ravine takes you to the beach. During storms, or on clear windy days, the breakers put on a dazzling display as they smash against the rocks. Exercise caution at high tide when "sneaker waves" sometimes roll in from far out on the sea and come all the way to the base of the cliffs. When the sea is rough, a high tide can roll huge pieces of driftwood onto the beach and up against the cliffs. Beached driftwood offers picnickers protection from wind, and pocket beaches provides shelter for sunbathers. Tidepools abound, making sea urchins, sea anemones, starfish, chitons and hermit crabs fascinating to observe, but remember collecting is prohibited. On calm days and at medium or low tides, McClures Beach is a perfect picnic spot. However, it is advisable to check at the Visitor Center, (415) 663-1092, for weather and tide information before going out to the beach.

POINT REYES BEACH NORTH and **POINT REYES BEACH SOUTH** are 13.2 miles and 15.9 miles from Bear Valley Trailhead respectively. These two beaches, which are two miles apart, are situated on the open sea along the Great Beach between Kehoe Beach and Point Reyes. One can drive to the beaches' edge at both locations. Restrooms and picnic tables are available at both beaches. The beach is narrow and the surf treacherous along the entire stretch of the Great Beach, so do not swim or even jump breakers at either of these Point Reyes beaches. You will find plenty of dunes, driftwood and space for picnicking. Dogs on leashes and campfires are allowed on the beaches.

MARSHALL BEACH is located on Tomales Bay and involves a 1 1/2 mile walk, including a steep trail, from the parking area to the beach. Drive from the Bear Valley Trailhead past Inverness on Sir Francis Drake Blvd. 7.5 miles to the junction and follow Pierce Point Road about 1.7 miles to the entrance to Tomales Bay State Park. Just past the State Park entrance there is a dirt road coming in from the right. This road, the Marshall Beach road, climbs abruptly through a conifer forest for 150 yards or more, and levels off in open country. 2.6 miles from Sir Francis Drake Blvd. you will come to the Marshall Beach parking area, which is marked with a sign. Along the Marshall Beach road you will observe some junctions with other ranch roads. Stay left and follow the Park Service signs directing you to the parking area. From the parking area it is 1.6 miles on an old ranch road to the beach.

The sandy beach is secluded, and usually less inhabited than the other beaches of Point Reyes National Seashore. Tomales Bay does not generally have a heavy surf or undertow and is, therefore, better for wading and swimming. However, Tomales Bay sometimes has sharks and there is no lifeguard on duty. Restroom facilities are available.

TOMALES BAY STATE PARK

Western shore of Tomales Bay. 3 miles north of Inverness, off Pierce Point Road.

The park features Coast Miwok Indian relics, Bishop pines, sandy beaches, many different species of plants, animals and birds. Park beaches are Shell, Pebble, Heart's Desire and Indian. There is fishing from shore, picnic tables and swimming. The water is around 68 to 70 degrees during the summer. A paved road leads to Heart's Desire Beach. Heart's Desire is considered one of the best family picnic beaches in the area.

Tomales Bay State Park is a preserve for the Bishop Pine. A memorial grove of the pines is dedicated to pioneer botanist Willis Linn Jepson.

- *8:00 am to 8:00 pm daily during summer.*
- *8:00 am to sunset during the rest of the year.*
- *Telephone: (415) 669-1140.*
- *$5.00 day use charge per vehicle*

POINT REYES BIRD OBSERVATORY

Mesa Road 4.5 miles north of Bolinas. 1/2 mile south of Palomarin Trailhead.

Open daily, April through summer. Otherwise open Wednesdays and weekends.

The Observatory is the only full time ornithological research station in the United States.

Birdbanding takes place early in the morning from April 1 through Thanksgiving.

Lookout Museum.   Special tours can be arranged by calling (415) 868-1221.

AUDUBON CANYON RANCH

Audubon Canyon Ranch is a wildlife sanctuary and center for nature education. It is located on Shoreline Highway approximately 13 miles south of Point Reyes Station.

   • *Open mid-March through mid-July. The public is welcome on Saturdays, Sundays and holidays 10 am to 4 pm*

   • *For appointments, or more information, call (415) 868-9244 or write: Audubon Canyon Ranch, 4900 Shoreline Highway, Stinson Beach, CA 94970.*

   • *No charge is made for visits, but contributions are welcome. They are needed for the maintenance and development of the Ranch and Nature Center and are tax deductible.*

Audubon Canyon Ranch contains a major heronry of Great Blue Herons and Great Egrets. Each year these birds nest in the tops of the tall redwood trees. They find fish and crustaceans for themselves and for their young in the water and tidelands of nearby Bolinas Lagoon.

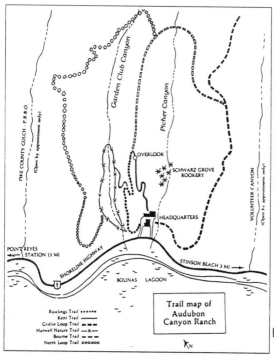

Trail map of
Audubon
Canyon Ranch

A steep 1/2 mile trail leads to Henderson Overlook. From the platform, at which telescopes are provided, you will enjoy a rare view into the nests of the Great Blue Heron and Great Egrets. A naturalist is at the Overlook to interpret the dynamics of the breeding colony and assist with the telescopes.

In 1969 the Ranch was designated a Registered National Natural Landmark by the Department of the Interior and the National Park Service for its exceptional value in illustrating the natural history of the United States.

GULF OF THE FARALLONES
NATIONAL MARINE SANCTUARY

The **Gulf of the Farallones National Marine Sanctuary** covers waters adjacent to the coast north and south of the Point Reyes Headlands between Bodega Head and Rocky Point and the Farallon Islands, including Noonday Rock. It encompasses approximately 948 square nautical miles. The shoreward boundary follows the mean high tide line and seaward limit of Point Reyes National Seashore. Between Bodega Head and the Point Reyes Headlands, it extends 3 nautical miles beyond state waters and includes the

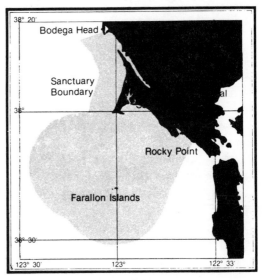

Gulf of the Farallones National Marine Sanctuary

waters within 12 nautical miles of the Farallon Islands, and between the Islands and the mainland from the Headlands to Rocky Point.

The Sanctuary was designated to protect an important part of our nation's marine resources.

The National Oceanic and Atmospheric Administration manages the

Sanctuary through the Sanctuary Programs Office of its Office of Coastal Zone Management. The program emphasizes the protection of special marine areas for the long-term benefit and enjoyment of the public. Research and educational programs have been initiated to improve our understanding and appreciation of the site's resources, and promote their wise use.

For additional information, contact:

Gulf of the Farallones National Marine Sanctuary
National Oceanic & Atmospheric Administration
telephone: (415) 551-6622

LIFEBOAT STATION

A visit to this National Historic Landmark structure helps one learn about the maritime and lifesaving history of the Point. The Lifeboat Station was used by the U.S. Coast Guard from 1927 – 1968. The first floor is wheelchair accessible with restroom.   Park at the Chimney Rock lot and walk a 1/2 mile down the paved road to the right, or take the shuttle on week-ends.

HOG ISLAND & DUCK ISLAND
ISLANDS OF TOMALES BAY

In the middle of northern Tomales Bay sit two small tree-topped islands. The big one (two acres) is Hog Island, and little one is called **Duck** (some call it Piglet) **Island**.

One story goes that **Hog Island** got its name after a bargeload of pigs, journeying from a Point Reyes ranch to the railroad line on the east shore of the bay, broke loose and deposited the pigs on safe ground. The name however, appeared on surveys well before the railroad was built. Photographs taken at the turn of the century show the island bare and grassy, with not one tree, looking a little like a wallowing hog. So true naming of the island still remains a mystery.

President Rutherford B. Hayes patented Hog Island to Christian F. T. Kuschert for "a few dollars" on August 20, 1878, and the island was known for many years a Kuschert's Island. The surrounding tidelands had been patented to neighboring entrepreneur James Preston in 1868. Duck Island was patented by President Chester K. Arthur to William Carmine in 1884. The two islands came under single ownership some time later.

Christian Hulbe and his wife raised a family in a wood frame home on the island in the 1880s. Because of the lack of a reliable water source, the Hulbes moved to a mainland home in nearby White Gulch, and by the turn of the century the house on Hog Island was gone.

In 1902 Kuschert gave Hog Island to his sister, Catherine, who soon sold the island to a sportsman named N. W. Mallery. It may have been Mallery who planted the eucalyptus, cypress and pine trees on the island. Mallery went bankrupt in 1909, and the following year Clara Windsor bought it for $800. The Windsor family owned Hog and Duck Islands for almost 60 years, allowing local boaters, fishermen and hunters unlimited access. Fred Windsor built the stone/concrete house and breakwater on the east shore in the late 1940s using island rock, and sand and granite from Tomales Point.

The Windsor family sold the islands for $55,000 in 1969. The new owners posted NO TRESPASSING signs which were immediately cut down by affronted locals. Three years later, Audubon Canyon Ranch took over, insuring that the islands would be kept in a natural state. In keeping with the island's traditional uses for recreation, youth groups, boaters and campers used the island with permission. Audubon Canyon Ranch long supported the addition of Hog and Duck Islands to Point Reyes National Seashore with the intent of continuing environmental protection and recreational use.

Today, as ever, access to Hog Island is by boat only. Pelicans abound on the sand point on the east side. At low tide visitors can walk on a natural sand causeway to Duck Island.

Now protected as a part of Point Reyes National Seashore, the islands are important habitat for harbor seals and other marine life.

Dead whale at beach below Arch Rock Overlook.

Marine Life

- *Elephant Seals • Harbor Seals • Sea Lions*

- *Coho Salmon & Steelhead Trout • Tidepooling*

- *Whales & Whale Watching*

- *Vantage Points • Eschricthius Robustus*

- *Terminology • Appearance Habits*

ELEPHANT SEALS

Elephant seals are in the process of establishing a new colony at Point Reyes. Here they can be observed from a safe distance for people and seals.

A new elephant seal viewing area has been constructed just a few hundred yards from the Chimney Rock parking lot. In January and February females are giving birth to 80 pound pups whom they will nurse for one month. Males are fighting for dominance and mating rights over harems of females. Expect brute force, guttural calls, fighting and quick retreats. Docents are stationed at the overlook on weekends to answer your questions. *Please do not approach within 100 yards of any marine mammal.*

Northern elephant seals spend, up to 300 days per year at sea. In the water, the elephant seal is a solitary creature who may dive a mile deep while hunting for nourishment. In their quest for food, females swim at least 11,000 miles and as far as the central Pacific Ocean.

Males journey 13,000 miles up the Gulf of Alaska for their meals. When the winter arrives, the seals are plump from their year of feeding and are ready to spend more time on land.

The first males come ashore in early December. Fat from their diets of skates, rays, and squid, they lumber onto the beaches using their front flippers. Males will congregate on the beaches and familiarize themselves with their competitors. Spending most of their time resting or engaging in mock battles, the males wait for the arrival of the first females.

A bit later in December the females begin to arrive, many of whom are pregnant from last year's mating. Females will group together in the colony for protection from the advancing males and for the protection of the pups. Shortly after their arrival, the female will give birth to a single pup. About twenty days after birth, the female will enter estrus for about four days and will allow one or several bulls to mate with her before returning to sea. Which bull is given the privilege is decided amongst the males.

Male elephant seals use aggression to establish dominance in the colony. Males will throw their heads back and bellow out a call. A bull that answers the vocalization must be prepared to do battle. Battles occur when a bull rushes another and the opponent accepts the challenge with equal vigor. Despite the bloody bites and forceful blows, death is rarely an outcome from these confrontations. Usually the loser is chased into the water with the victor nipping at his retreating flank and the issue is settled.

After weaning the pup, the females return to the ocean to feed and the males soon follow. After many weeks ashore, the fasting elephant seals have lost as much as one third of their body weight. Pups remain at the colony for 8-12 weeks longer, perfecting their hunting and swimming skills,

Because of the length of time northern elephant seals are at sea and because of the extensive distances which they travel, little is known about their habits in the water.

Beach closures will be in effect during pupping season. Check at visitor centers for more information. If you are interested in learning about northern elephant seals consider joining the Point Reyes Elephant Seal Docent program.

VIEWING ELEPHANT SEALS

- *Main viewing area is from Chimney Rock around headlands to Great Beach.*

- *Shuttle buses are available from Drakes Beach on weekends December through April ($2.50 per person, children under 12 free).*
- *Ranger, docent-led walks on weekends. Telephone (415) 663-1092*

- *Point Reyes Field Seminars offers guided day trips and outings. Telephone (415) 663-1200.*

HARBOR SEALS

Harbor seals *(Phoca vitulina)* are distinguished from other species of seals and from sea lions by their dark and light spotted coats and their lack of external ear flaps. Their average length when grown is about five feet, and males and females are nearly identical. They can be found along the Pacific Coast from the Bering Sea to Baja California, sometimes hauled out on the Seashore in large numbers. Because they are non-migratory, they may be seen year round.

Seals and sea lions haul out because they cannot maintain their body temperature if they stay in the cold water all the time. On land, they can absorb the heat from the sun. Their preferred hauling grounds are sandy beaches, mud flats, and reefs. Many of the beaches and mud flats along Point Reyes National Seashore are popular hauling out spots for the harbor seals. Pupping season here occurs from March into May, during which time the number of seals present at any given time at the hauling sites reaches a peak.

While hiking along the wild wet shores of the Pacific in the spring, you may come across a seal pup alone on the beach. Don't assume that it has been abandoned. If you see a lone pup, inform the Park Service of your observation, but do not touch or move the pup. The mother is probably in the water nearby feeding. It is very difficult to reunite a mother and pup after the pup has been moved, and practically impossible to raise a pup in captivity.

A harbor seal pup can swim at birth but pups are almost always born on land. Pups are born with thick fur that insulates them from the cold until they put on weight. Although mother seals are extremely attentive, they will frequently leave a newborn pup on the beach while they seek food. When she returns from feeding, the mother will groom, caress and nuzzle her baby pup constantly, as well as nurse it with her extremely rich milk. The rich milk (about 48% fat) helps the pup to put on weight rapidly. When the pup can swim faster the mother will keep it close by her until the time of weaning, at around two months.

Harbor seals are extremely sensitive to disturbance. They may leave their hauling areas temporarily — or even permanently — after harassment by people, boats or aircraft, or other equipment. Historically they have abandoned hauling sites altogether due to a high incidence of human disturbance, as was the case in San Francisco Bay. To help preserve this sensitive and unique creature, people should take care not to make their presence known either visually or audibly when they come across an individual or group of harbor seals, as the seals may flee into the water immediately when they sight a human.

The Marine Mammal Protection Act of 1972 includes harbor seals, along with sea lions, whales, porpoises, sea otters, and other mammals, under federal protection. This law prohibits killing or harassing these shy creatures in any manner. Any human action that causes a change in the behavior of a marine mammal is considered harassment.

March marks the beginning of the Harbor seal pupping season. Watch for the mottled seals as they swim along Limantour Beach or bask on secluded sandbars at low tide. Typically, they are the shyest of the seals and the most sensitive to human disturbance. Keep at least 100 yards away from any beached seal. *To protect their breeding habitat, Drakes Estero is closed to all boating from March 15 - June 30.*

Training for volunteers interested in assisting with harbor seal monitoring begins in January and February. Telephone (415) 663-8522 x 224 for information.

SEA LIONS

A staircase at the Sea Lion Overlook has been constructed allowing visitor access to a viewing area for California and Steller sea lions. A small platform is reached by descending a short set of steps. Even when heavy fog obscures the views, the deep barking calls and the pounding of the surf reverberate up the rock face. Though the sea lions do not breed here at the seashore, they do utilize the remote, rocky beaches to haul out, warm up and rest almost year round. The overlook is located just before the Lighthouse parking lot.

COHO SALMON • STEELHEAD TROUT

For thousands of years coho salmon and steelhead trout have returned from the vast ocean feeding grounds to the shaded streams of their birth. Look for salmon one to three days after a rainstorm. Traditionally, January is the best month to spot the spawning coho and steelhead. *Use caution in the sighting areas. Watch out for stinging nettle and poison oak.* Please remember, viewing is safest and most protective of the environment from bridges and trails.

For information about becoming involved in the **Coho Salmon and Steelhead Trout Restoration Project**, call (415) 868-0732

WHERE TO VIEW COHO SALMON & STEELHEAD TROUT

Leo T. Cronin Fish Viewing Area — Shafter Bridge — Lagunitas Creek: On Sir Francis Drake Blvd. at the eastern boundary of Samuel P. Taylor State Park. From December through the end of February the Marin Municipal Water District opens a parking area next to the bridge to facilitate fish viewing. Marin Municipal Water District Sky Oaks Ranger Station (415) 459-5267.

Samuel P. Taylor State Park: At the entrance station to the state park just off Sir Francis Drake Blvd., there is a short, steep access trail to the creek's edge where you may see fish swimming upstream. Samuel P. Taylor State Park (415) 488-9897.

Devil's Gulch in Samuel P. Taylor State Park: A few miles west of the entrance is the Devil's Gulch tributary of Lagunitas Creek. Access the trail on the north side, across from the pull out on Sir Francis Drake Blvd. A flat walk takes you along the creek, providing several spots from which to view fish. Samuel P. Taylor State Park (415) 488-9897.

Olema Creek, Five Brooks Trailhead: On Highway One, approximately three miles south of the intersection of Highway One and Sir Francis Drakes Blvd. Park at the trailhead and follow the driveway back towards Highway One. On the right side, follow the path to the creek's edge. Point Reyes National Seashore (415) 663-1092.

Redwood Creek, Muir Woods: Highway One to Frank Valley/Muir Woods Road will take you to the entrance of Muir Woods. Park in the lot provided then proceed on foot following the path through the entrance gates ($2 entrance fee) and along Redwood Creek. Check the park schedule of ranger programs for an opportunity to learn more about the spawning salmon. Muir Woods National Monument (415) 388-2595.

TIDEPOOLING

Tidepooling can be a great deal of fun for families and anyone who wishes to explore a unique ecosystem. The best and most successful time to go on a tidepool adventure is at a negative low tide.

Though the tide cycles two times a day, it is not always at the same level. The level of the tide depends on the spacial relationships between the sun, moon, and the earth. *Tide tables are available at the visitor centers or at local book and sporting goods stores.* A two hour window of time, starting one hour before and ending one hour after the stated low tide, is the safest time for exploration.

Always keep one eye on the waves and the water level to make sure you are not surprised by an unexpected wave surge or trapped by the incoming tide in a secluded spot. Sculptured Beach is a good spot to go tidepooling. Chimney Rock is closed during elephant seal pupping season.

Tidepools are very fragile and a refuge for the special creatures found there. It is against the law to remove living organisms from tidepools. Examine, enjoy, and then replace carefully where they were found. Resist the temptation to collect.

WHALE WATCHING

During their southern migration along the western coast of North America, whales seek waters much closer to the shore than they would otherwise. This effort, by the calving mothers, to avoid the high seas, makes them extraordinarily visible. The migration begins in mid to late December, and is usually at its heaviest in January. In February there are fewer whales, and by March one sees only a few stragglers. Since whales swim at a speed of three to five miles an hour, their progress is easily charted.

When watching for whales at Point Reyes National Seashore one must consider the best vantage points, and when one is most likely to see whales.

VANTAGE POINTS

- Point Reyes itself. The most commanding view is near the Point Reyes Lighthouse.

- On the Coast Trail some 300-600 vertical feet above Miller Point. An excellent view of Drakes Bay.

- On the Woodward Valley Trail, at the point where the trail breaks out into the open at 500' above sea level. Face the ocean, then look 45 degrees to your right to a small nearby

Whale watching at Point Reyes near the lighthouse.

hill some 50 vertical feet higher than where you are standing. Walk 100 yards to the top of this hill.

• Along the Coast Trail near Wildcat Beach, there is a spot amid pine trees, near some old boarded up forts. Just past the pine trees, there is a dramatic view of Drakes Bay.

• Along the Coast Trail, in the first two miles north of Palomarin Trailhead, there are places with a good view of the ocean.

• Along the Coast Trail from where it crosses Coast Creek and where it turns inland towards the Hostel there are a number of locations just west of the trail where one can have a good view of Drakes Bay. Above Kelham Beach, at the promontory of Point Resistance, above Secret Beach, and above Sculptured Beach.

A good pair of binoculars is recommended for anyone searching for whales at Point Reyes National Seashore.

Dress warmly, as it will probably be windy and/or foggy at the Lighthouse. The Lighthouse area is really very wind. You would do well to call the Lighthouse Visitor Center in advance for a weather and whale activity report, (415) 669-1534.

The Oceanic Society Expeditions offer naturalist-guided whale-watching out of San Francisco and Half Moon Bay. Baja Expeditions can bring you close up and sometimes within touching distance of Grays. Call Whale Watch (415) 474-3385.

ESCHRICTHIUS ROBUSTUS

This is the best known of the great whales in California, and the one most often seen. Gray whales feed in the summer, in the western Bering Sea and Arctic Ocean in the winter.

The grays migrate down the Pacific Coast from Alaska to Baja. There, in various of the bays and lagoons of Baja California and the mainland (most notably thr Scammon Lagoon) the females have their calves and breed. Gestation is 13 months. Later, in March and April, they reverse the route, plying their way back up along the coast— only this time not quite as close to the land.

They travel to Baja fairly close to the shore, often coming within a few hundred yards of some points, or even into the surf zone.

The grays travel around 13,000 miles on their round trip, and the trip takes 2 1/2 months. The distance is calculated to be 60 to 80 nautical miles per day, at a speed of 4 knots for a 15 to 10 hour day. They frequently raise their heads out of water to look around and get their bearings. Whales are believed to find their way on the long migration by memory and vision.

TERMINOLOGY

Spouting.   The visual release of vapor from the air held in the lungs under great pressure and therefore cooled.   The vapor has quite a smell. Also called blowing.

Pod.   A group of whales, all the way fro, 3 or 4 to 20 or 30, traveling together.

Breaching. To leap out of the water.

Baleen Whales. One of two groups of whales, the other group is toothed. These whales have no teeth. Instead, they have sheets of a fringed horny material, hanging from their upper jaws. They use this to strain out plankton. It is interesting that the largest of all animals feed low on the food chain, at a level where food is most abundant.

APPEARANCE

Gray whales reach 35 to 50 feet in length and around 20 to 40 tons in weight. The calf is 15 to 16 feet long at birth. Females produce one calf every two years, at the most.

The whale is black, mottled with gray, and covered with barnacles and whitish scars. There is no dorsal fin, but there is a small, distinct ridge on the back, at about the location where a fin would be, followed by a series of bumps.

A thick layer of fat or blubber helps the whales combat the cold ocean water.

Whales have almost lost their hair, but not quite. A gray whale has over 100 hairs on its chin and the tip of its upper jaw.

HABITS

The gray whale, one of the baleen whales, feeds mainly on small crustaceans, though to some extent on small fish as well. Feeding takes place largely, it is believed, during the four months of the year spent in the north. There is some evidence of feeding during the eight months spent in migration and in the lagoons.

Sleep is accompolished by taking short naps, while the whale drifts motionless near the surface. The gray whale, sleeping in the lagoons, breathes every 5 to 10 minutes.

Whales have a sophisticated method of communication consisting of clicks, hums, whines, whistles, etc. This is often called "singing."

The whale is hunted for its oil, its bone and for food. The toll on the whales has been so heavy that it has threatened their continued existence. In 1938 an international agreement giving the gray whales complete protection, and regulating the taking of whales, was put into effect. The gray whale is an excellent example of how a formerly endangered species can flourish under complete protection. However, the fate of many whale species is precarious.

In October, the cold winter waters force the gray whales south and away from their nutrient-rich feeding grounds in Alaska. Headed for warmer water and the safe birthing bays in Baja, they begin to pass Point Reyes in late December. The largest number occur in mid-January. On a clear, calm day you may see dozens swim by the Point. Look for the opaque white spout which rises about 12 feet as they exhale. Once this is spotted, use you binoculars for a glimpse of the back. Often after 3 or 4 blows you will see the fluke (tail) come up for a last heavy push, sending the whale further along its 10,000 mile round trup migration.

The best months to watch for the grays on their return trip is March and April when mothers and calves hug the coastline, providing for closer views.

More information about whales and whale migration is available from the following organizations in California:

General Whale, Alameda & Oakland	(510)865-5550
Greenpeace, San Francisco	(415)512-9025
Oceanic Society, San Francisco	(415)441-1104
Lawrence Hall of Science, Berkeley	(510)642-5132
The American Cetacean Society, San Pedro	(213)548-6279
Marine Mammal Center, Sausalito	(415)289-7325

The Oceanic Society has a **Field Guide for the Gray Whale** available. Call for ordering information.

Birds

BIRDS

More than 450 species of birds inhabit the Seashore at one time or another, much to the delight of birdwatchers.

Seabirds include gulls, cormorant, murres, pelicans, ducks, egrets and loons. Other birds include pigeons, hawks, kites, wrens, woodpeckers, turkey vultures, nut hatches, flycatchers and jays.

In the fall and winter, the wetlands of Estero de Limantour are a haven for migrating shorebirds and waterfowl. Greater Yellowlegs, Green-winged Teals and Ring-necked Ducks can be seen.

During the winter, Hooded Mergansers and Wood Ducks may be spotted in the quiet seclusion of Fivebrooks Pond.

Migrating waterfowl may be seen at Drakes Estero.

BIRDWATCHING

Point Reyes National Seashore offers some of the finest birdwatching in the United States. More than 70,000 acres of habitat harbor an incredible variety of bird life. Over 450 avian species have been observed in the park and on adjacent waters.

The park's coastal location and its wealth of unspoiled habitats — estuaries, grasslands, coastal scrub and forest — all attract many migrating and wintering birds. The projection of the peninsula some 10 miles seaward from the geologic "mainland" make Point Reyes

National Seashore a landing spot for many vagrants—birds that have made errors in navigation and thus are unexpected in this area.

All these factors account for the Point Reyes area consistently reporting one of the highest tallies in the nation every year during the Christmas bird count.

Five Brooks Pond. In winter, green-backed heron, hooded merganser, ring-necked duck, and grebes can be seen. In grasses and trees watch for pileated woodpecker, swallows, accipiters, warblers, and thrushes.

Bear Valley. A great variety of land birds frequent the numerous habitats along the trails over Inverness Ridge to the ocean—warblers, sparrows, kinglets, thrushes, wrens, woodpeckers, hummingbirds, crossbills, and owls.

Olema Marsh. The largest fresh water marsh in Marin County supports marsh, water and riparian species including belted kingfishers. At high tide, egrets and herons feed on rails and voles.

Tomales Bay and Bolinas Lagoon. Important for wintering waterfowl including three species of scoters and Brant geese; osprey, shore birds, herons and egrets all year.

Tomales Point. Outstanding for finding birds of prey during fall and winter months. In winter look for owls, peregrine falcons, and hawks. Passerines feed on seeds and insects in this area.

Abbotts Lagoon. Excellent for winter ducks and raptors. Black-shouldered kites are commonly seen in winter and fall. This is also a sensitive nesting area for the endangered snowy plover.

Please tread carefully on the sandy beaches during the spring and early summer months.

Estero Trail.   An old pine plantation provides winter roosting habitat for long-eared and great-horned owls. Look for water and shore birds such as great egrets, great blue herons and loons in the Estero. Watch for hawks above the grasslands.

Drakes and Limantour Estero.   Abundant water, shore and marsh birds including grebes, herons, egrets, terns and loons.

Outer Peninsula Grasslands.   Look for winter vagrant ground dwellers including plovers and longspurs and migrating and resident hawks. Watch along the roadside for flocks of perching birds.

Ranchlands.   Dairy ranches are Seashore property leased back to the ranchers. *Please respect property rights and privacy.*   Avoid buildings, gardens and farmyards. Leave all gates just as you find them and do not block any gates with cars. Consider carpooling to these areas in order to reduce traffic congestion. In spring and particularly fall, see unusual vagrant passerines and raptors.

Lighthouse rocks and cliff areas.   Brown pelicans in fall, numerous pelagic and migrating species in spring. Most common spring pelagics include cormorants, common murres, pigeon guillemots, loons, and scoters. Keep your eyes out for black oystercatchers all year. Peregrine falcons are occasionally spotted. Tufted puffins are occasionally seen in the spring and early summer.

BIRD WATCHING OPPORTUNITIES

Check the visitor centers for specfic times for the following:

Birds of Abbotts Lagoon: Wander through a mixture of ecosystems looking for raptors, song birds and wintering waterfowl. Dress in layers. Bring binoculars, field guide and drinking water. Meet at Abbotts Lagoon parking lot. 2 hours.

Birds of Bear Valley: Hike some of the loop trails in the vicinity of the Bear Valley Visitor Center in search of resident and migrant birds. Easy walking. Bring field guide and binoculars. Meet at the Bear Valley Visitor Center. I hour.

Birds of Drakes Bay: This is a quiet beach, hugged by white sand cliffs where one can watch both land and shorebirds. Meet at the Ken Patrick Visitor Center with binoculars and field guide. 1.5 hours.

Birds of Five Brooks Pond: A gentle, 1/2 mile loop offers a unique opportunity to see secretive waterfowl and forest-dwelling songbirds. Bring binoculars and field guide. Meet at Five Brooks trailhead. I hour.

Birds Of Estero de Limantour: Explore the wetlands of Limantour, a haven for migrating shorebirds and waterfowl. Bring your binoculars and field guide. Meet at the Limantour Beach parking lot. 2 hours.

WATERFOWL

Winter is the time of year to become more familiar with waterfowl, such as Northern pintails, Gadwalls, American wigeons and Ring-necked ducks. Tomales Bay, Abbotts Lagoon, Bolinas Lagoon and Muddy Hollow Pond are just a few of the areas they can be found.

As spring approaches, waterfowl return to more northern haunts and we are serenaded by the songs of arriving neotropical migrants to the forests, woodlands and riparian corridors of the peninsula. Bird journals are kept at visitor centers for recent and unusual sightings.

SNOWY PLOVERS

The western snowy plover is a small, pale colored shorebird with dark patches on either side of its upper breast. This bird is easily mistaken for the more common sanderling, which is often seen chasing the waves up and down the beach.

The nesting season of the snowy plover lasts form mid-March to late-August. With the onset of spring and summer crowds, nests are destroyed by the unintentional trampling by humans, horses and unleashed dogs. Plover nests consist of just a scrape in the sand and their eggs are small, spotted, and well camouflaged against the tan, grainy expanse. Although the greatest threat to these little birds has been from predators such as ravens, humans have played a major role in their declining numbers.

In 1993, the U. S. Fish & Wildlife Service listed the western snowy plover as a federally threatened species. Researchers at Point Reyes National Seashore and at Point Reyes Bird Observatory are working to save this tiny beach visitor from extinction.

Fences are put up around nest sites to protect eggs from predators. These predator exclosures have dramatically improved their hatching and fledgling success rate.

MURRES

Though common murre populations were decimated by egg collectors after the California gold rush, and again in the 1980s when approximately 75,000 were killed by gill net fishing, you can still see these sturdy, black and white birds breeding on the rock below the Lighthouse.

In 1986, a combination of commercial gill net fishing and the Apex/Houston oil spill wiped out the breeding colony of over 3,000 murres at Devil's Slide Rock south of Pacifica. Court settlements for damages incurred by the spill have enabled rehabilitation work at Devil's Slide. No breeding is believed to have occurred on this rock since 1986. As part of a 10 year project, the murre population at Point Reyes will be used as a control site to monitor and compare the return of the Devil's Slide colony.

The birds return to nest on or near the same rock. In subsequent years they will not only return to the same rock, but to the same spot on that rock to breed. This is why the work at Devil's Slide Rock is so crucial. Breeding for murres begins at 4 - 6 years of age. Each season a pair lays only one pear shaped egg. The shape of the egg ensures that if it rolls it will only go around in circles and not over the edge of the cliff. The low egg number allows a better success rate for the young, but does not provide for a quick recovery of population.

In mid-July when the fledgling is only about 1/4 of its adult weight, it leaps off the breeding rock and onto the ocean, followed by its father. The father continues to feed the young bird for about two months. This time on the water together has two purposes. First, it allows the parents to expend less energy feeding their young since they do not have to fly back and forth to the top of the rock and second, the adults can go through a molt (during which it cannot fly) without sacrificing care of the young. Propelled by their wings, murres forage for fish by diving up to 180 meters below the ocean's surface.

Today's main threats include oil spills, disturbance from low flying aircraft, plastics, pollutants. They are especially unsafe around the drift nets which entangle millions of various sea birds each year.

Overall, common murre numbers in California are making a slow comeback. They have recently been listed by the state as a "species of special concern".

THE SPOTTED OWL

Hikers at dusk may be treated to the unusual "barking" calls of the rare spotted owl. Although endangered throughout most of its

Spotted owl. Photograph by Stephan Meyer.

range, the spotted owl finds refuge in Marin County. Due to the county's unique heritage of use and protection, these denizens of the night are found in many of the deep, shady and cool canyons of the Seashore. If you are fortunate to find the day roost of these large nocturnal predators. approach quietly to observe and you may find them equally curious about you! Point Reyes contains the highest density of spotted owls in the world.

SWAINSON'S THRUSH

A common summer resident of Point Reyes is the Swainson's thrush. Its musical song can be heard almost everywhere. The Swainson's thrush is a neotropical migrant, spending the majority of its life in the rainforests of Central America. There, they join mixed-species flocks of small birds and will often follow swarms of army ants, hoping to prey on insects fleeing from the path of the ants. Each spring, the thrush journeys to the temperate zones of North America to breed. While in the Seashore, it eats the blackberries and huckleberries that grow along the hiking trails. However, it feeds its nestlings protein-rich insects. Once the young have been raised, the Swainson's thrush returns to the tropics.

Wildlife

Female Tule elk

WILDLIFE

There is a great variety of animal life in the Point Reyes National Seashore area. There are no bears in Bear Valley, in spite of the name.

Thousands of **Tule elk** were in the area before 1860. The small free-roaming herd of Tule elk that was reintroduced north of the old Pierce Ranch has experienced a population boom. Since the Tule Elk herd at Tomales Point has grown rapidly in recent years, the National Park Service scientists and managers are studying such options as relocation of part of the herd and birth control methods. Tule Elk can be dangerous during rutting season. Heed the warnings of the signs. Tule elk are year round residents. Young bulls and elk calves may be seen in May. The Pierce Point Road ends at the Tule elk range.

Deer to be found at the seashore are black-tailed deer, the white fallow deer and the Indian axis deer.

Jack rabbits, pocket gophers, squirrels, badgers, skunks and brush rabbits abound.

Racoons and foxes can be pests at the campsites, and campers should protect their food by using the food lockers provided.

Also found inhabiting the Seashore are coyotes, bobcats and mountain lions in the remote areas near Palomarin and the Tomales headlands.

An Annotated Checklist of Mammals of Point Reyes National Seashore by Gary M. Fellers and John Dell'Osso is an excellent reference on mammals. It is available at the Visitor Center.

NATIVE & EXOTIC DEER

When traveling through Point Reyes National Seashore deer are a common sight. The Seashore has three wild and reproducing species of deer living within its boundaries. Occasionally they intermingle when feeding, but they do not interbreed.

black-tailed deer

The native black-tailed deer (*Odocoileus hemiounus columbianus*) are distributed throughout the 100 square miles of the Seashore. They can be seen any time of the day, but evening brings many deer out to feed in open pastures where they are more visible.

Although they are often seen in large temporary feeding groups, black-tailed deer do not form herds. Unlike other deer, the black-tailed do not migrate and may spend their entire life within the same area.

In October, the bucks enter rut, or mating season, and gather the females into harems for breeding. Fawns are born in April and May, and are covered with white spots for the first three and a half months. Does will establish a territory to protect their fawns from other females. If startled, a fawn will lie down in the brush while the doe attempts to draw off a predator. The absence of scent further protects a growing fawn.

Every year the bucks shed their antlers around January and begin to grow new ones the following spring. The covering of velvet which provides the antlers with food and oxygen is rubbed off in early fall. Despite popular belief, the number of points on a set of antlers does not indicate the age of the buck.

The exotic axis deer *(Axis axis)*, or chital, are native to India and Ceylon. Introduced by Dr. Millard Ottinger, a San Francisco surgeon, who also operated a ranch on the west side of Mount Vision, eight were brought in from the San Francisco Zoo in 1947 and 1948. Today their numbers are estimated to be between four and five hundred. The axis deer range from McClures Beach in the north, to Estero de Limantour in the south.

Axis deer are the most sociable of all deer and may be seen in herds as large as 75 to 100. Their native name of chital refers to the white spots which are visible all year against their reddish-brown coat. They are further distinguished by the dark stripe running the length of their back, and the white "bib" present.

axis deer

The bucks carry long antlers that are forked at the top, with another fork near the base. Antlers are shed in the winter.

Fawns of all sizes are seen throughout the year, indicating that impregnation and birth occur during all seasons. The axis deer feed and hide in the coastal scrub, but are often grazing in open grassland. When alarmed, a loud, sharp "yowp" is given that alerts the herd. If danger is close, the herd takes off usually led by a mature doe.

Fallow deer *(Dama Dama)* are native to the Mediterranean region of Europe and Asia Minor. In England, noblemen traditionally kept

semi-domesticated fallow deer in their deer parks, where centuries of selective breeding produced numerous coat colorations. Colors range from white to buff to charcoal with lighter underparts, and brown with white spots. Fallow deer in America stem from the English stock. The color type of an individual deer does not change through its lifetime.

fallow deer

Fallow bucks have large, palmate antlers much like those of moose. The older bucks tend to herd separately from the does, except during the rut in October. Their antlers are not shed until April and the velvet of the new antlers is shed in August. Fawns are born in mid-June, rarely occurring as twins. A fawn is often a different color type from its mother.

Between 1942 and 1954, 28 fallow deer were purchased from the San Francisco Zoo by Dr. Millard Ottinger. Today their population is estimated at about 500. They have spread as far south as Double Point, and as far north as Tomales Bay State Park.

Recent studies on the exotic deer indicate that their population numbers are increasing. Unchecked populations result in competition for forage with native black-tailed deer. Due to this potential problem, the National Park Service has initiated a program of exotic deer management. This management program consists of continued research to determine the optimum population levels, and deer reduction to keep the population within these limits. The selective deer reduction is performed by Park personnel.

MOUNTAIN BEAVER

Tending its network of tunnels, the chunky burrowing mountain beaver *(Aplodonta rufa)* is seldom seen by people. The mountain beaver is not a beaver, nor is it partial to mountains. It is, however, like the pronghorn, the last surviving species of its family, and unique to North America. Until about a million years ago they lived throughout the western United States.

A mountain beaver looks like a muskrat with no tail. It weighs two or three pounds. Found only on the Pacific slope from Marin County north to British Columbia, it likes dense woods or shrubby tangles near water. It eats only plants, and almost any plant will do. Sword ferns are a favorite. Look for a burrow six to ten inches wide, with an opening the size of a softball, hidden under a clump of swordfern. This is just one stop on a subway system up to 300 feet long kept up by a single animal. At each stop, food is cut and carried below to be eaten or stored. Mountain beavers do not hibernate. When winter rains flood their tunnels, they splash on through. Babies are born in March or April, two or three per mother. Within three months, the young tunnel off on their own.

MOUNTAIN LIONS

Mountain lions *(Felis concolor)*, also called cougars, roam throughout the Point Reyes peninsula and adjoining park lands, and have long been a part of the landscape of west Marin.

Wildcat Camp was named for the once frequent sightings of mountain lions. Today, though they have been seen in campgrounds and along hiking trails, it is rare for park visitors to encounter one or be injured by these secretive animals.

The reclusive behavior of mountain lions and their tendency to live in remote areas explains why we know little about these graceful cats which once ranged from northern Canada through South America and from coast to coast. Due to hunting and loss of habitat since the 1920s, mountain lions are now seen predominantly in western states.

Mountain lions establish home ranges that average 25-30 square miles. These home ranges may overlap, since female lions often establish a range adjacent to their mothers. Lions restrict their hunting, breeding, and raising young to these specific ranges. If a lion is unable to establish a range in its first three years, it will probably die.

For the first year, cubs are spotted for camouflage and stay close to their mother's den. They hunt with their mother until by the age of two they begin to wander out of the maternal range, seeking to establish their own territory.

Sighting a majestic lion is a rare treat. Generally, there is no need to fear lions.

However, *if you should encounter a lion, follow these guidelines:*

- If you have young children, do not allow them to hike or walk ahead of you. If you encounter a lion, pick small children up.

- Do not run. Mountain lions associate running with prey and may chase you. Hold your ground, or move slowly away while facing the lion.

- Do not crouch down; try to appear as large as possible.

- If the lion behaves aggressively, wave your hands, shout, and throw sticks, packs, etc. at it. This action protects you and "teaches" the lion that humans are not good prey.

REPTILES

The western garter snake, gopher snake, and yellow-bellied racer are the snakes commonly found at Point Reyes National Seashore. Rattlesnakes are less common. Lizards found include the southern alligator lizard, western fence lizard and western skink. Other reptiles found at the Seashore are the Pacific pond turtle and California newt.

THE MONARCH BUTTERFLY

As days shorten and get cooler in the fall, the monarch butterflies throughout the western states begin flying to the Pacific Coast. They will gather in the same sites monarchs have used for generations. Hundreds of these dramatic black and orange butterflies have been known to cluster November through January in the eucalyptus trees at the Palomarin Trailhead. Look for them out sunning themselves or sipping nectar when the morning light warms the trees.

Vegetation

Vegetation Overview • Landscape & Cover Type • Wildflowers • Bishop Pine • Mushrooms

VEGETATION OVERVIEW

ALONG THE BEACHES AND ESTEROS

grasses • marshy plants • bush • beach strawberry • lizard tail•
gum weed • coastal bush lupine (yellow) • sand verbena • wind
swept shrubs, particularly abundant coyote bush

INLAND GRASSLANDS

berry plants • poison oak • shrub • lupine • mustard • California
poppy • Indian paintbrush • Douglas iris • tidy tips• monkey flower
• morning glory • brodiaea • blue-eyed grass • suncups• sneeze
weed • goldfields • buttercups • blue eyes • blue grass

INVERNESS RIDGE AREA

Douglas fir • Bishop pine • California laurel • maple• tan oak •
coast live oak • madrone•   alder   Pacific dogwood • Pacific
bayberry • California buckeye • western yew • manzanita • poison
oak • blue huckleberry • California coffeeberry • red and blue
elderberry • salmonberry • thimbleberry • nettle• forget-me-nots •
milkmaids • shooting stars • cow parsnip

Point Reyes has a number of endemic species and several rare and
endangered species of wild flowers. An example of a variety of a
wildflower found nowhere else is the yellow form of meadow foam.

LANDSCAPE & COVER TYPE

The flora of Point Reyes National Seashore shows that the peninsula has long been the meeting ground of northern and southern

Baytree arches

California Coast Range floras. A forest of Douglas fir grows on the eastern slopes of Inverness Ridge and in some of the deeper canyons facing the ocean. Bishop pines, unique to the California coast, occur on the northern half on the Inverness Ridge. A small grove of coast redwoods in the southern part of the Seashore adds to the ecological variety. Mingled with the Douglas firs, or flanking them at lower levels, are groves of broadleaf trees consisting of madrone, California bay, tanbark oak, live oak, maple and red alder. A profusion of shrubs includes rhododendron, ceanothus (wild lilac), honeysuckle, wild rose, wax myrtle and black huckleberry. Woodland is interspersed with grassland in which the California buckeye is a common and conspicuous feature. The ranges of five species of plants are confined exclusively to the Point Reyes peninsula. Two endemic manzanitas grow only on Mount Tamalpais and the peninsula.

On the seaward side of the ridge the brush covered slopes of the hills include thickets of chaparral-type growth. Wind-swept coastal bush lupines, kinnikinnick, gumweed, sea thrift, coyote brush, and succulent plants live on the maritime bluffs. The small valleys in the brushlands contain islands of coast live oak and wind-pruned California bay. Some twenty-five species of shrubs grow on the sides of these brushy hills. Coyote brush is a common colonizer and may occur as an almost pure stand. Poison oak is omnipresent in both brushland and woodland. A versatile plant, poison oak may occur as a clump or thicket three or more feet high, or as a vine climbing up tree trunks, or as a ground runner.

The rolling lowlands facing the sea are covered with extensive grasslands. A profusion of wildflowers decorates the area in springtime. Much of the grassland may be due largely to agricultural practices. Over the years the land has been plowed, planted to crops, and then seeded to non-native grasses for pasture. Stock grazing for more than a century has drastically altered the native grassland complex. In the pastoral zone grow many exotics; Monterey cypress and blue gum eucalyptus are fairly common in the Seashore.

Along the dunes and beaches the dramatic see-saw struggle of plants to bind the shifting sands and establish themselves in spite of wind and waves is a fascinating ecological story. Many of the dune plants, particulary the lupines, produce a notable wildflower spectacle. Since the introduction of European dune grass and ice plant, the flora and topography of the sand dunes has changed dramatically. Some plants unique to the dunes of Point Reyes must be carefully monitored to insure their protection.

The fresh water marshes, although of limited extent, are of great interest to plant ecologists. The swales lying behind sand dunes which have dammed natural drainages produce a distinctive group of spring plants.   The salt water marshes, with growths of pickleweed and sea-blite, are vital feeding grounds for a great variety of waterfowl. As a result of the diversified plant life and climate, the wildlife of the peninsula shows a corresponding diversity, ranging from salt water shore birds to the birds and mammals typical of dense mountain forests.

WILDFLOWERS

Expect to see wildflowers beginning to bloom as early as January in some coastal areas, though the peak usually occurs in March and April. Sites to consider for flower forays are *Tomales Point, Abbotts Lagoon, Chimney Rock* and areas on the *west side of Inverness Ridge, such as the Bucklin* and *Woodward Valley Trails*, where the Vision Fire burned in October 1995.

Please remember, wildflowers must not be picked.

Flowers of Point Reyes National Seashore by Roxana S. Ferris (1970) is an excellent field guide and reference.

Wildflowers of Point Reyes National Seashore, published by the Point Reyes National Seashore Association, features 60 of the most common wildflowers seen in park. Excellent full color photographs. Proceeds support park resource management and education programs. Copies are available ($5.00) at Visitor Center bookstores or by mail by calling (415)663-1155.

BISHOP PINE

The Bishop pine (*Pinus muricata*) forest at Point Reyes is one of the last descendants of a once widely distributed closed-cone pine forest which existed here about one million years ago. Scientists theorize that the forest evolved in Mexico during the Miocene Epoch, 12 to 26 million years ago, and has been transported north through tectonic forces along the San Andreas Fault. Today, there are only seven separate populations of Bishop pines scattered along the coast of California. Their populations occur adjacent to areas of marine upswelling and persistent fog. For the Bishop pine, this fog is a vital source of precipitation necessary for survival.

The Bishop pines are found growing primarily in soil derived from granite. Granitic rocks form the backbone of the peninsula and are exposed along the northern portion of Inverness Ridge from Tomales Point to Mount Wittenberg. Geologists think that the granite here originated in the Tehachapi Range in the southern Sierra Nevada Mountains near Santa Barbara, California.

The Bishop pine is known as a closed-cone pine because it depends on outside stimuli for seed dispersal. Fire is the cones' strongest stimulus. These types of cones are called "serotinous". Flames melt the resin coating that glues the scales together. Sometimes age, the heat from the sun or insect damage can open the cones as well. Once the cones open, the seeds drop and germinate if conditions are right. The conditions that fire leaves behind are ideal for this germination — bare mineral soil enriched with newly released nutrients from burned duff and wood, plenty of sunlight, and low competition from other plants.

There is much evidence to suggest that fire has been an integral component of the peninsula's ecosystem for millions of years. The native plants have evolved adaptations that allow them to survive periodic fire. The Bishop pine is an example of a plant that has directly benefitted from the Vision Fire of October 1995. Adult Bishop pines, by design, are not adapted to withstand fire. The high concentration of resins make them highly flammable and its thin bark offers little protection. The mature trees are largely killed or severely weakened to make room for a plethora of tiny seedlings, giving birth to a new forest. This growth pattern results in "same age" stands. Bishop pines have relatively short lives of up to 100 years of age. The adults we see today on the ridge are largely the result of a fire which occurred in 1927.

Closed-cone pines can maintain seed viability for up to thirty years. Cones remain airtight and anti-oxidants contained in the scales and seed coats keep unsaturated seed oils from becoming rancid.

This story of regeneration and replacement can be witnessed on Inverness Ridge where the Vision Fire burned at a high intensity. The existence of Bishop pines at Point Reyes attests to the fact that fire had been an important force in the evolution of life here on the edge.

MUSHROOMS

Mushrooms vary in size and shape from delicate creamy white *fairy parasols* to more common brown colored **Inky caps.** They sometimes cluster along a rotting log or climb the bark of a Douglas Fir tree along the Bear Valley Trail. The fir forest is a haven for mushrooms, as is the Bishop Pine forest of Inverness Ridge. The forests and slopes are full of the elements mushrooms need: rotting wood, moisture and tree roots. WInter is the best time to see mushrooms.

Long prized for their tasty flavors, mushrooms play a largely unknown role in the health of the forests. Recent studies have indicated that certain species of trees need mushrooms amongst their roots in order to remain healthy.

Recently, many parks have experienced an increase in mushroom harvesting because of their commercial value in the culinary market. This increased harvesting brings an, as yet, unmeasured impact as soil is disturbed and plants are uprooted and damaged.

Careful harvesting of mushrooms is permitted at Point Reyes, and an individual may collect one quart of mushrooms for personal use.

Use caution in harvesting and eating mushrooms. Be sure to correctly identify the species you are collecting to ensure it is safe to eat. Pick a few at several sites instead of clearing a whole area; mushrooms are clustered together because they share common root systems. Leaving part of the cluster allows the plant to rejuvenate itself.

Recreational Activities

- *Bicycling* • *Canoeing* • *Kayaking*
- *Fishing* • *Saltwater Invertebrates*
- *Hunting* • *Horseback Riding*

BICYCLING

Bicycles are prohibited within the wilderness areas. Bicyclists should check at one of the visitor centers about trail use and restrictions.

Over 35 miles of trails are open to bicycles at Point Reyes National Seashore, and over 10 miles more in the adjacent Golden Gate National Recreation Area. Stop by a visitor center to pick up a free trail map which defines these areas. Remember safety, courtesy and respect for the wilderness while on these trails.

- When on a bicycle trail, travel no faster than 15 miles per hour and slow down around blind curves. Bicyclists yield to both hikers and horses.

- Bicycles are not allowed off-trail or in designated wilderness areas, nor may they be walked or carried while on pedestrain trails.

- Bicycles are not allowed on the Earthquake Trail, the Woodpecker Trail or at Kule Loklo.

- Cyclists found not adhering to these rules will be cited and their equipment possibly confiscated.

KAYAKING

Kayaking is a magical means of exploring the mainly inaccessible Point Reyes coastline, discovering isolated beaches and observing the area's abundant wildlife. Conditions can change rapidly and the tidal influence is strong, so this activity should not be done alone by beginners. Fortunately, the myriad opportunities and ease of access have encouraged several rental shops and guide services to become estanlished.

• Plan a day to explore the westside of Tomales Bay — Heart's Desire Beach. Tomales Bay State Park is a good place to launch. *White Gulch and Beach* is a good lunch spot. A hike up is often rewarded with good views of tule elk.

• Kayaking at Abbotts Lagoon is for the hardy. The put in is over a mile from the parking lot. Once there, a gentle exploration of the watery environment and abundant waterfowl is rewarding.

• Launching from Johnson's Oyster Farm allows for a full day of paddling in Drakes Estero and exploring the finger bays. Watch for stingrays and leopard sharks on the estero bottom. There are many pocket beaches for a leg stretch or lunch.

• If you are looking for a little adventure on the ocean in an area that is still protected, try Drakes Beach!

FISHING

Regulations. People 16 years of age and older must have in their possession a valid California fishing license for the taking of any kind of fish, mollusk, invertebrate, amphibian, crustacean or reptile (except for rattlesnakes). No amphibians or reptiles may be taken. *All* those who are fishing are responsible for adhering to all *fishing hours, limits, methods and other fishing regulations* found in the pamphlet *California Sport Fishing Regulations,* obtainable at stores selling fishing licenses, bait and equipment. Regulations are strictly enforced. **Caution:** *Regulations may be very specific to certain areas. You must refer to the sport fishing pamphlet to obtain that information.*

RESTRICTED AREAS. **Point Reyes Headlands Reserve** and **Estero de Limantour Reserve** are set aside as **reserves** and **all** marine life is protected within their boundaries. In the **Duxbury Reef Reserve,** *some* invertebrates and fish can be taken.

- *Fishing in all creeks and streams within the Seashore is prohibited.*

- Refer to fishing regulations for specific information. Maps showing boundaries of reserves and fishing areas are available at visitor centers.

- There are no public fishing piers within the Seashore.

Protect sea birds: sea birds are being caught in fish hooks and are becoming seriously hurt.

Here is how you can help:
- Do not throw used fishing line into the water.
- Watch your bait at all times, and make sure sea birds do not grab your bait.
- If your hook becomes tangled do not cut the line, untangle it by hand.
- Do not fish near roosting areas.
- Use biodegradable hooks and supplies.
- Take your garbage for disposal in refuse cans.

SALTWATER FISH — See "California Sport Fishing Regulations" for specific regulations.

> **Drakes Bay** — flounder, sea trout, perch, leopard shark and rockfish.

> **Tomales Bay** — flounder, halibut, jack smelt, lingcod, redtail perch, salmon, striped bass, sturgeon and trout.

> **North and South Beaches** — serf perch, flounder, sea trout. Beware of extremely heavy surf.

> **Sharks** — angel, sevengil, sand, leopard and great white sharks have been taken in Drakes and Tomales Bay. No season, no limit, all sizes.

> **Poke Pole Fishing** — done in tide pools along Palomarin Beach, McClures Beach, and other rocky shores for blenny eels and rockfish.

FRESH WATER FISH — See "California Sport Fishing Regulations" for specific regulations.

> **Trout, Bass, Bluegil, Crappie** — Many reservoirs and lakes in the Seashore were stocked in the past when under private ownership. While the National Park Service has not restocked them, fishing remains fair in some of the lakes. Fishing is allowed in some creeks and streams within the Seashore.

> **Nearby Fishing Areas** — Nicasio Reservoir, Lagunitas Creek (Papermill Creek) below the Highway 1 bridge (closed Oct. 1 - Dec. 31), Walker Creek below the Highway 1 bridge.

FISHING ACCESS — Access to many areas within the Seashore is limited. Many areas can be reached only by foot trails, and some beaches only by boat. Parts of the northern grasslands are still operating ranches. Please respect the rights of these ranchers when crossing pasture lands.

SALTWATER INVERTEBRATES

See "California Sport Fishing Regulations" for specific regulations.

Invertebrates may not be taken from any tidepool or from any other area between high tide mark and 1,000 feet beyond low tide mark in Point Reyes National Seashore, except for: abalone, chiones, clams, cockles, crabs, lobsters, rock scallops, sea urchins, native oysters and ghost shrimp. Mussels may be taken in all areas except in State Park System Reserves or Natural Preserves.

Quarantine — From May 1 through October 31, the California State Department of Health places annual quarantine on mussels and occasionally Washington clams. During this period, mussels and the dark part of all clams and scallops may concentrate a toxic material that is highly poisonous to humans. Only the white meat of clams and scallops should be prepared for human consumption. Check with the park visitor centers if you have any questions.

   Clams — one-half hour before sunrise to one-half hour after sunset.

   Gaper *or* **horseneck** — Tomales Bay and Drakes Estero. Limit: 10.

Washington —Tomales Bay and Drakes Estero. Limit: 10.

Geoduck — mouth of Tomales Bay. Limit: 3.

All gaper, Washington and geoduck clams dug, regardless of size or broken condition, must be retained until bag limit is reached. *Please refill holes after digging to reduce damage to environment.*

Cockles — Tomales Bay and Drakes Estero. Minimum size: 1 1/2 inches in greatest diameter. Limit: 50.

Mussels — McClures and Kehoe Beach. Limit: 10 pounds.

Oysters — cultivated and sold commercially in Drakes Bay and Tomales Bay.

Abalone — Palomarin Beach, McClures Beach, Tomales Point. Minimum size: Red abalone, 7 inches; Black abalone, 5 inches. Limit 4. All legal size abalones detached must be retained and detaching shall stop when bag limit is reached. Season: April-June, Aug.-Nov. Hours: 1/2 hour before sunrise to 1/2 hour after sunset only.

Crabs — Tomales Bay. Red rock crabs, minimum size: 4 inches. Limit:35. Season: all year. Dungeness crabs, minimum size: 6 1/4 inches. Limit: 10. Season: 2nd Tuesday in November through June 30.

HUNTING

Hunting is not permitted. The use of firearms, air guns, or weapons of any kind is prohibited. This also applies to fireworks.

HORSEBACK RIDING

Horses are permitted in the Seashore area, with certain restrictions. A map is available at the visitor center which outlines designated trails on which horses are permitted. Horses may be rented at Five Brooks Stables (415) 663-1570 or Stewart's Horse Camp (415) 663-1362. Inquire about guides.

The Bear Valley Trail region, is open to the horseback rider as well as to hikers. About 70 miles of well-marked trails are available to riders. The same regulations that apply to saddle and pack animals in other national parks and recreation areas are in effect at Point Reyes.

Horses and other saddle or pack animals are permitted only on those trails or routes established for their use, except in those areas were cross-country travel is permitted by the Superintendent, such as along Santa Maria and Wildcat Beaches.

The use of horses or other saddle or pack animals upon the main roadways is prohibited except where such travel is necessary for entry to or egress from the trails, or is incidental to authorized travel.

In the interest of public safety and welfare, the Superintendent may require that saddle horse parties and/or pack trains shall be in charge of a licensed guide or other guide who meets qualifications which may be established by the Superintendent.

Riding horses or hitching horses in the campgrounds, in picnic areas, in the vicinity of eating or sleeping establishments or other areas of public gatherings *is prohibited.*

Riders shall slow their horses to a walk or slow trot when passing persons on foot or on bicycles.

At Point Reyes National Seashore these additional rules were established for the safety of all visitors:

- Horses may **not** be ridden on the Bear Valley Trail passed the Mt. Wittenberg junction, Meadow Trail, or Old Pine Trail on Saturdays, Sundays, or holidays.

- Horses may **not** be ridden on the Woodward Valley Trail, the Estero Trail, Coast Trail between Arch Rock and Wildcat at any time.

- Horses are **not** allowed on the Earthquake Trail at any time.

- Horses may **not** be ridden on Drakes Beach.

- The National Park Service asks that you not smoke while you are on a horse. Find a clear spot without flammable vegetation and dismount to smoke, being careful to break matches and extinguish all coals.

Wildcat Camp and Beach from the Coast Trail

Overnight Accommodations

• *Camping in Point Reyes National Seashore*
• *Point Reyes Hostel • Recommended Equipment
List • Campgrounds Outside of Point Reyes
National Seashore • Bed & Breakfasts*

CAMPING IN POINT REYES NATIONAL SEASHORE

RULES, REGULATIONS & GENERAL INFORMATION

• Camping is restricted to the four backpack campgrounds. Within each campground, there are specific, numbered sites for which permits will be issued. Camping is limited to four nights per visit with a maximum of 30 nights per year. If no group site is available, we will not split up a group into several sites due to the pressure on the resources. This policy protects the Park for future enjoyment by others.

• No dogs or other pets are permitted.

• Wood fires are prohibited in the campgrounds. Only gas stoves, charcoal or canned heat may be used for cooking. Downed wood may not be gathered and burned. Driftwood fires are permitted on sandy beaches below the high tide line. Permits are required for beach fires in the park and can be picked up with your camping permit. **Put fires out with water, not sand.**

• Camping must be within your designated campsite. You may not camp on beaches.

• No firearms (including air guns), fireworks or other potential weapons allowed. Quiet hours are from sundown to sunrise. Respect your neighbor and the wilderness.

• Campsites should be left clean. Pack out all trash.

• Maximum number of horses or pack animals in any campground is eight. Horses are not allowed at Glen Camp. Pack animals and horses must be tied to hitch rails.

TIPS —

Store your food properly in the food lockers. Do not leave any food unattended or stored in your tent. Raccoons, foxes and skunks are plentiful and aggressive. **Do not feed wild animals.**

SAFETY —

• Sleeping on beaches is both dangerous and prohibited.

• Do not climb cliffs. Stay back from cliff edges. They are sandstone and crumble easily, leaving no foothold.

• To reduce encounters with ticks, stay on trails and out of grassy or brushy areas. Wear light colored clothing and check it frequently.

• Poison oak and stinging nettles are common and abundant plants here. Stay on trails to help avoid them. Ask at the visitor center for information if you do not know how to recognize these plants.

• All park animals are wild. Do not attempt to touch or feed them. Report stranded or wounded animals, or mountain lion sightings, to a ranger on patrol or at a visitor center. Do not attempt to touch or move injured animals!

• All marine animals are protected by law. Stay at least 100 yards away.

BACKPACK CAMPING INFORMATION

Camping is by permit only: Camping permits must be obtained at the Bear Valley Visitor Center before starting your trip. Camping is allowed only in one of our four established campgrounds in the site specified on your permit.

Reservations are strongly suggested: Telephone reservations will be accepted only between the hours of 9:00 am and 2:00 pm , Monday through Friday at (415)663-8054. Reservations will not be accepted at any other time over the phone, but reservations will be taken at any time in person. Campgrounds can be reserved up to two months in advance. For example, one can make reservations for May 1 on or after March 1. Weekends and holidays can fill up quickly, especially for group sites.

Camping fee: The cost is $10.00/site/night for sites of up to 8 people and $30/site/night for group sites for 9-25 people. A credit card is required for phone reservations. Payment is due at the time the reservations is made. There is no longer the need for check in times or calls to confirm. Once payment has been made, the site is yours for that period of time. However, a permit must still be picked up before beginning your trip. Those arriving after 5:00 pm, after the visitor center has closed, should look for their permit in the after hours box on the information board in front of the building.

CAMPGROUND RESERVATION SYSTEM

Point Reyes National Seashore

Phone: (415) 663-8054

Hours: Mon - Fri 9 am - 2 pm

Fees: $10/night individual/family site (1-8) people)

$30/night group site (9-25 people)

CAMPSITES

Each campground has a water faucet and a pit toilet. Each campsite has a picnic table, food storage locker and charcoal brazier. Drinking water may not always be available due to well conditions. Even though new wells have been drilled. Check with the Visitor Center for current water conditions at your site, since they will vary. If the water is not drinkable treat, it must be treated with iodine tablets, boiling for one minute or filtering with a commercial filter.

Glen Campground is in an inland clearing surrounded by Douglas firs and oaks and a nearby stream. It is 2 trail miles from Wildcat Beach.

- 12 individual campsites for 1-8 people each.

- No groups over 8 people allowed.

- No horses or pack animals allowed.

- 4.5 miles from Five Brooks or Bear Valley trailheads.

- Bike access from Five Brooks, 4.5 miles— strenuous.

Wildcat Campground rests in an open flat near a small stream that flows to the sea and is a short walk to Alamere Falls. Primarily a group campground, there are a few individual sites.

- 2 individual sites for 1-8 people each.

- 3 small individual sites for 1-4 people each.

- 3 group sites for 9-25 people each. Wildcat is the only camp where 2 group sites may be reserved for up to 40 people.)

- When not reserved by groups, the sites make 6 individual sites for 1-8 people each.

- Maximum 8 horses/pack animals overnight.

- 5.5 miles from Palomarin, and 6.5 miles from Five Brooks and Bear Valley trailheads.

- Bike access is from Five Brooks trailhead on Stewart Trail, 6.5 miles — strenuous.

Sky Campground sits inland on the western side of Mt. Wittenberg, at an elevation of 1025 feet, with a view to the ocean on clear days. A few sites are in an open grassy area, others are within the brush or trees.

- 12 individual sites for 1-8 people each.

- 1 group site for 9-25 people.

- Maximum 8 horses/pack animals overnight.

- 1.7 miles from Sky trailhead on Limantour Road and 3.2 miles from Bear Valley via Mt. Wittenberg Trail.

- Bike access from Sky trailhead, 1.7 miles--moderate.

Coast Campground is on an open bluff about 200 yards from the south end of Limantour Beach near the tidepools of Sculptured Beach. Many sites are in an open grassy meadow, some are in a semi-protected valley of brush.

- 12 individual sites for 1-8 people each.

- 2 group sites for 9-25 people each.

- Maximum 8 horses/pack animals overnight.

- 1.8 miles from Laguna trailhead:2.3 beach miles from Limantour parking lot: 2.8 miles from Coast trailhead: 5.8 miles from Bear Valley via Mt. Wittenberg or 8.0 miles via Arch Rock.

- Bike access on Coast Trail from near the Youth Hostel, 2.8 miles– easy.

RESERVATION PROCEDURES

Decide when and where

• Decide what dates and which campgrounds you wish to reserve. Have an alternate trip planned in case your first choice is already booked full.

• Check the *Camping Update Line*, Ext 400 to see if your choice is still available.

• Remember, part of the wilderness experience is planning your trip, not just taking it.

• *Be ready when you make the call.*

Be Prepared!

• Prepare the form *below* as a guide for yourself when you call. The reservationist will need to know all this information when you call.

• Being prepared saves time--for you as well as for others waiting on the line to make their reservations. Please be courteous.

• All reservations for dates after July 1 must be paid for in full at the time of the call.

• *Be ready when you make the call.*

Make the call

• You may make reservations up to two (2) months in advance. (For example, you may call May 1 for camping on July 1.)

• **By phone**, you may call to make reservations Monday through Friday from 9 am to 2 pm. Call (415) 663-8054 for reservations.

• No reservations are taken after 2 pm by phone.

• Calls are processed in order at the capacity of our phone system and staff.

• You may make only one reservation of up to 4 nights per call.

• **In person**, you may come to the Bear Valley Visitor Center to make reservations Monday through friday 9 am - 5 pm or Saturdays, Sundays and holidays from 8 am to 5 pm, within the two month time limit.

Reservations/Cancellations
• Mon-Fri 9 am - 2 pm (effective. May 1)
• (415)663-8054

Bear Valley Visitor Center

• (415)663-1092
• Camping update: Ext 400

Fees:
• $10/night per individual site (max. 4/8 people)
• $30/night per group site (max. 25 people)
• Golden Age/Access Card holders receive a 50% discount. Card holder must be camping. All fees must be paid in full at the time the reservation is made.

Refunds &Cancellations
• Absolutely no refunds will be given.
• If you call to cancel by *2 pm the last weekday before* your reservation you may take that one time to reschedule another available date.

RESERVATION FORM

Have information ready on this form before you call:

1. Number of people in party (Include all adults and children over 3 years olds.):_____

2. Traveling by: _____ foot _____bike _____ horse (Total # of horse/pack animals:_____

3. Organization Name/Troop # (mandatory if applicable):_____

_____

4. Name of person picking up permit:_____

5. Daytime Phone: (_____)_____

6. Address _____

_____

7. Golden Age/Access Card Number _____

8. Payment will be by: MasterCArd or VISA #:

_____

Experiation date:_____ Name on card:_____

9. Flyers requested to be sent with confirmation letter

_____ Mountain Biking

_____ Trail Riding & Pack Animals

_____ Campgrounds in Marin County and laong the North Coast

_____ Others _____

First Choice						**Second Choice**					
	Date	Coast #	Sky#	Glen#	Wlldcat#		Date	Coast #	Sky#	Glen#	Wlldcat#
1st night						1st night					
2nd night						2nd night					
3rd night						3rd night					
4th night						4th night					

RECOMMENDED EQUIPMENT LIST
For Overnight Excursions To
Point Reyes National Seashore

---

1. all items recommended for day hikes, except that a pack frame and bag are preferable, in my opinion, to a knapsack

2. sleeping bag -- Coast Camp and Wildcat Camp are especially damp. The cold nightime air and high humidity mean dew. A fiberfill bag is somewhat preferable to a down bag in these circumstances. Yet down works satisfactorily, especially if one sleeps inside a lightweight tent. If one doesn't have any kind of tent, then it is better to sleep under trees (plenty at Glen Camp and at Sky Camp, but hardly any at Coast or Wildcat Camp). However, if it's a very foggy night, the trees will drip so it is my recommendation that one sleep inside a tent or tube tent.

3. tent or tube tent — I strongly suggest that the tube tent be erected by first running it through a nylon cord, both ends of which are tied to nearby trees or firmly established stakes. A lightweight camping tent is infinitely preferable to a tube tent, but the latter is much cheaper.

4. some stoves we recommend as efficient and light include: *MSR Whisper Light* white gas burning, *Whisper Light International* white gas & kerosine burning, *GAZ 270/Turbo* attaches to 270 or 470 GAZ ISO butane canister.

5. ensolite or foam pad — 4' length of 1/2" x 3/4" pad to insulate you from the hard ground at night.

6. ground cloth — an 8' x 3' plastic ground cloth is recommended only if you aren't going with tent or tube tent.

7. *lightweight* cooking pots, griddles, fry pans adequate to the

cooking needs at hand — Stirring spoons, ladles, spatulas as needed.

8. cup, spoon, fork, plate — all lightweight

9. scouring pad and biodegradable soap

10. matches — Carried in a plastic bag, sealed.

11. flashlight — Disengage the batteries for travel on the trail, lest you have a dead battery upon reaching camp.

12. food — Planned for economy of space and weight.

POINT REYES HOSTEL

Point Reyes Hostel
P.O. Box 247, Point Reyes Station, CA 94956.
(415) 663-8811.
Office hours: 4:30–9:30 p.m. &   7:30–9:30 a.m.

HOSTELLING
INTERNATIONAL

Located in a secluded valley in Point Reyes National Seashore, this country hostel is a haven for hikers and a retreat for individuals or groups wanting a quick getaway from the city.

The Hostel.   The Point Reyes Hostel is located two miles from Limantour Beach, and is accessible by car, foot, or bicycle. Once a working ranch house, the Hostel offers all the amenities of a large vacation cabin, including a spacious, fully-equipped coountry kitchen, dining room, common area, hot showers, and an outdoor barbecue and patio. Hostelers share friendship, adventures and lively conservations in the two common rooms warmed by woodburning stoves. Up to 44 guests can enjoy moonlit nights sleeping soundly either in the main ranch house or the redwood bunkhouse. There is also a family room available in the main house.

Limited wheelchair accessibility. Please contact the hostel for complete information.

Rates:

$12-$14 per person

$1.00 per person linen rental

Half price for children accompanied by parent.

Midweek discount offered to school groups during off-season.

Hosteling Customs. Hostelers around the world follow a few simple customs. Hostelers provide their own food, towels, soap and sleeping bag. Here, you are part of a community where everyone lends a hand after breakfast by doing a simple cleaning chore. It is this self-help system which allows hostels to be inexpensive and offer a friendly, cooperative spirit. Check-in hours are between 4:30 p.m. and 9:30 p.m.; the hostel is closed between 9:30 a.m. and 4:30 p.m. The use of intoxicants is not permitted on the premises, smoking is allowed outside the hostel only, and pets are not allowed. And, as in most hostels, travelers may stay a maximum of three days.

Groups. The Point Reyes Hostel is well suited to group use. In the past, hiking clubs, Girl Scout troops, photography seminars, bodywork seminars, bicycling groups, senior social clubs, religious retreats, youth outing groups, and many informal gatherings of families and friends have used the facility. A group of 20 or more can be guaranteed exclusive use of their own private redwood bunkhouse with large common room and fireplace. Write or call as soon as you begin to make your plans.

Getting to the Hostel. From Highway 101 going north from San Francisco, take Sir Francis Drake Blvd (heading toward San Anselmo) to Olema. At the blinking light in Olema, turn right onto HIghway One and go 100 yards north and turn left onto Bear Valley Road. Make the second possible left hand turn (approximately 1 1/2 miles) at Limantour Road (unsigned). Follow Limantour for about 5 1/2 miles and turn left at the first crossroad (bottom of a very steep hill). Coming from the north on Highway 101 exit at Petaluma and take the Point Reyes-Petaluma Road to Point Reyes Station and go south on Highway One to Olema then follow the same directions as above. Call the hostel or stop for directions to Point Reyes-Petaluma Road. The only bus service to the area is on weekends and it arrives at the Bear Valley Visitor Center near Olema. It is an 8-mile hike from the Visitor Center to the hostel.

Reservations. Try to make reservations as far in advance as possible. To secure a reservation, a deposit of the first night's fee for all members of your party is required. Reservations can be made by check through the mail or with a Visa or MasterCard. If reserving by mail, please specify genders and children's ages. The one family room can only be reserved by people with a child aged 5 years or younger. Call the hostel during office hours (7:30-9:30 am) and 4:30-9:30 pm) to check availability. Do not leave messages on the answering machine. For information on how to make a group reservation (8 or more people) please call the hostel.

Cancellation & Refunds.   At this hostel, a full refund will be given to individuals who make a cancellation 72 hours or more before their arrival.   No refunds or date changes can be made with less than 72 hours notice. For group reservation, cancellation and refund policies please contact the hostel.

CAMPGROUNDS
OUTSIDE POINT REYES NATIONAL SEASHORE

Olema Ranch Campground	(415) 663-8001
Samuel P. Taylor State Park	(415) 488-9897
Mount Tampalpais State Park (walk-in)	(415) 388-2070
Lawson's Landing (Dillon Beach)	(707) 878-2443

BED & BREAKFASTS

Bed & Breakfast Cottages of Point Reyes	(415) 663-9445
Coastal Lodging of West Marin	(415) 663 1351
Inns Of Points Reyes	(415) 663-1420
Point Reyes Youth Hostel	(415) 663-8811
Seashore Bed & Breakfast	(415) 663-9373
West Marin Chamber Of Commerce	(415) 663-9232
West Marin Network	(415) 663-9543

Point Reyes Educational Programs

- *Clem Miller Environmental Educational Center*
- *Point Reyes Seminars* • *Camps for All Ages*

CLEM MILLER ENVIRONMENTAL
EDUCATIONAL CENTER

Point Reyes Educational Programs is a project of the non-profit organization, Point Reyes National Seashore Association in cooperation the National Park Service.

For information on any of the *Point Reyes Educational Programs*, please write:

Point Reyes Educational Programs
Point Reyes National Seashore
Point Reyes, California 94956 (415) 663-1200

The Education Center is an overnight outdoor facility which can accommodate up to 80 people. The main building is a new 4600-square foot cedar building with two large classrooms, including various teaching aids and study materials, an extensive library and some nature exhibits. The main building also houses a large kitchen. There are six dormitory cabins and a central restroom building. The Clem Miller Center is available as a resource to groups wishing to develop an awareness, understanding, and appreciation for their environment. Located in a meadow at the foot of a Douglas fir by a canyon, the Center is surrounded by hiking trails and is just two miles from the great stretch of beach at Limantour. A newly developed nature trail at the Center provides a short exploration through a forested valley.

POINT REYES FIELD SEMINARS

The Point Reyes Field Seminars program conducts courses within Point Reyes National Seashore in natural history, photography, environmental education and the arts, all taught by recognized professionals. By offering educational opportunities which utilize the tremendous resources available within the seashore, they strive to foster in others an understanding of, concern for, and desire to preserve the health of the natural environment. A non-profit, self-supporting program, they are a division of the Point Reyes National Seashore Association in cooperation with Point Reyes National Seashore.

Point Reyes Field Seminars offer a wide variety of courses in natural history, environmental education and the arts. The courses are taught by recognized professionals, and many offer optional credit through Dominican College of San Rafael.

The program is a self-supporting non-profit activity, sponsored by the Point Reyes National Seashore Association in cooperation with Point Reyes National Seashore.

The seminars,which meet at Point Reyes National Seashore, are offered throughout the year.

For further information, or to be placed on the mailing list, write Seminar Coordinator, Point Feyes Field Seminars, Point Reyes, California 94956; or call (415) 663-1200.

CAMPS FOR ALL AGES

Summer Camp.   Five-to-eight day sessions of summer camp provide boys and girls between seven and twelve years old with and in-depth perspective of the Point Reyes National Seashore. Traditional camp activities such as canoeing and backpacking are offered along with salt water marsh study, tidepool investigation, and bird and mammal observation.

Adventure Camp.   A one-week Adventure Camp challenges teenagers (thirteen to sixteen years of age) to test their potential in the natural environment. Activities to choose from may include: a three-day canoe voyage to Tomales Bay, backpacking to the far corners of the National Seashore, rock climbing and horseback riding.

Elderhostel.   Elderhostel is an international program for people over 60 years old combining the best traditions of education and hosteling. Elderhostel at Point Reyes provides a unique opportunity to learn about the fascinating Point Reyes peninsula, combining intellectual stimulation and physical adventure.

Environmental Awareness

• *What's Being Done* • *Ways You Can Help*
• *Ways To Become Involved*

WHAT'S BEING DONE

• **Behind the Scenes** The brown colored toilet paper in the park's restrooms may stand out. This is post consumer recycled paper. Point Reyes is integrating post consumer recycled products and environmentally friendly or bio-degradable cleaning products such as simple green into daily use. The absence of paper towels in the restrooms and presence of hand blowers further supports the Park's waste reduction efforts. Park employees also reuse and/or recycle products used in park operations including cardboard, paper, styrofoam, oil and oil filters. An energy audit was recently done by PG&E of the administrative headquarters offices. It was discovered that simply by using a different type of florescent light bulb in overhead fixtures over 70% of the energy requirements for lighting the two buildings could be saved.

• **Car Wash** A closed system car wash is now used for cleaning park equipment and vehicles. The water used while washing is collected and filtered through a system which traps oils and other particles washed off vehicles. This same water is then available to wash the next vehicle and the oils are kept from draining into creeks. No soap or wax is used.

• **Waste Management** The objective of the Dairy Waste Management and Reclamation Project is to demonstrate an innovative and reliable method of managing and reclaiming dairy wastes that can reduce water pollution and adverse impacts to watershed quality while improving the economic performance of the dairy. The three year project will be based at Kehoe (Historic J) Ranch off of Pierce Point Road. Wastes from the dairy will be managed in such a way that methane produced from the fermentation of solid wastes will be used as an alternative energy source to off-set the farm's energy needs. Nitrogen from waste will be reclaimed in the form of protein rich algae from a pond designed to optimize green algae growth. The algae produces oxygen for the pond necessary for the breakdown of wastes, and can then be harvested, dried, and used as protein-rich feed supplement.

• **Power Sources** The original, overhead electrical power system providing service to the Limantour and Laguna Ranch areas of the park has been replaced from Sir Francis Drake Blvd. to the Muddy Hollow area. The 1995 Vision Fire seriously damaged this 3.5 mile segment which passes through the wilderness area and follows the route of a historic ranching road. Because of the intensity of the burn along this route, the potential for severe erosion exists for several years. Slope stabilization projects will follow the removal of overhead power lines and poles.

Electrical service is now provided to the Limantour area by conductors, placed underground, out of sight, along Limantour Road.

This project accomplished several objectives: 1) removal of man-made features from a Wilderness Area, 2) improved the visual aesthetics and reliability of service to the area, and 3) preserved a historic ranching road from further erosion.

• **Trash Containers** New animal-proof trash containers have been installed at all visitor centers and most visitor use areas throughout the park. Unfortunately, these cans frustrate some humans as well as wild animals when they attempt to open them. These containers are aesthetically pleasing and eliminate the unsightly results of animals rummaging through garbage.

WAYS YOU CAN HELP

Be a responsible park visitor

• **Stay on Trails** Avoid crushing seedlings or compacting soil by staying on the trails and not taking shortcuts.

• **Respect "Area Closed" signs** These closures reflect concern for safety and for the long term health of the wilderness. The Park Service asks your cooperation in allowing them, nature and time to help restore trails and stabilize slopes.

• **Garbage & recycling** — Check out the green metal "animal proof" bins located at parking areas throughout the park. Some bins are for garbage and others are for recycling. You can recycle tin and aluminum cans in the bins marked "aluminum" and #1 and #2 type plastic containers (look on the bottom of the container) as well as glass in the bins marked "glass". By using products that have minimal packaging or are in containers you help reduce the amount of trash in the park.   Pack out your trash from wilderness areas and campgrounds when possible.

• **Do not feed the animals at the seashore** — The food which animals are fed or tend to scavenge is not only unnatural, but often unhealthy and possibly harmful over the long term.

• **Things to keep in mind** —
  • Watch your step! When walking, jogging or horseback riding on the beach, nests could accidentally be destroyed.

  • Before venturing out with your dogs, check the rules to ensure pets are allowed, and make sure dogs remain leashed.

Trampling of nests by unleashed dogs is unintentional but does happen. More importantly, dogs love to chase birds, causing stress to an already fragile animal, especially during the nesting season. Dogs also leave the scent of a predator where ever they roam.

• Take part in keeping beaches free of garbage. Trash attracts hungry predators to beaches.

WAYS TO BECOME INVOLVED

• *"Adopt A Trail" Program*
In an effort to combat budget cutbacks and restrictions which could jeopardize trail conditions at Point Reyes National Seashore, an "Adopt a Trail" program was launched.

The program encourages groups and organizations to *adopt* one of the park's trails, and provide maintenance at least two weekends a year. Work includes drainage and trail surface repair and water bar maintenance.

Tools, materials and general supervision will be provided.

For more information, call Point Reyes National Seashore Park Headquarters at (415) 663-8522.

• *Volunteer with the Habitat Restoration Team*
The Volunteer Habitat Restoration Team meets twice a month on weekends to control the spread of non-native plants, such as Scotch and French broom, pampas grass and crocosmia well as monitoring burned areas for plant regrowth and assisting with a variety of reha-

bilitation projects. Invading non-native plants have played a role in the decline of the snowy plover habitat all along the California coast. Not only do these plants invade open areas, they provide cover for predators like ravens and foxes. Call (415)663-1092 ext. 432 for more information or to sign up.

Taxpayers have spent billions of dollars purchasing and protecting wildlands that are now being lost due to invasion by non-native plants. 17.5% of the flora in California is exotic (non-native plants). On federal lands alone, it is estimated that non-native plants are claiming 4,600 acres every day and dominate over 17 million acres in the western United States. 1.9 million invasive non-native plants were removed from the National Seashore in 1996. Call (415) 663-1092 ext. 432 to volunteer.

• Become A Member of the
Point Reyes National Seashore Association
Since 1964, the Point Reyes National Seashore Association has worked in partnership with the National Park Service to preserve and protect the natural and cultural resources of Point Reyes National Seashore. The Association has allocated funds for projects such as protecting the nests of the federally threatened western snowy plover from raven predation, reversing the effects of damming and silation of streams to provide spawning grounds for the federally threatened coho salmon, and surveying and researching the expanding tule elk population on Tomales Point.

Annual membership benefits include mailing of the park newspaper, a 15% discount on visitor center purchases and invitations to special "members only" events. To receive membership information call (415) 663-1155 or write the Point Reyes National Seashore Association, Point Reyes, CA 94956.

Directory

• *General Services* • *Education Centers*
• *Communications* • *Telephone For The Hearing Impaired* • *Emergency* • *Service Stations*
• *Bank/ATM* • *Campgrounds* • *Rentals For Recreational Activities* • *Where To Stay*
• *Where To Eat* • *General Stores*
• *Oyster Companies* • *Bakeries*
• *Newspaper* • *Galleries* • *Special Events*

GENERAL SERVICES

Information Centers
Bear Valley Visitor Center   (415) 663-1092
Bear Valley Weather, Whale, & Info   (415) 663-9029
Ken Patrick Visitor Center   (415) 669-1250
Lighthouse Visitor Center   (415) 669-1534

Coin Laundry
Olema Ranch Campground   (415) 663-1041

Post Offices
Olema   (415) 663-1761
Point Reyes Station   (415) 663-1305
Inverness   (415) 669-1675

EDUCATION CENTERS

Point Reyes Field Seminars   (415) 663-1200
Point Reyes Bird Observatory   (415) 868-1221
Marine Mammal Center   (415) 331-7325
Marin Wildlife Center   (415) 454-6961

COMMUNICATIONS

Radio As you drive out to Point Reyes National Seashore tune
your car radio to 1610 AM to hear updated Park Information. You

will hear of weather and traffic conditions, special events, natural history notes, and naturalist activities.

Recorded Weather & Information (415) 663-9029

On The Internet Parknet www.nps.gov

TELEPHONE DEVICE FOR HEARING IMPAIRED

Bear Valley Visitor Center   (415) 663-1092

EMERGENCY

All Emergencies Call   **911**

Medical Services
West Marin Medical Center   (415) 663-1082
Point Reyes Clinic   (415) 663-8666

SERVICE STATIONS

Inverness
Drake Highway Garage   (415) 669-1017

Point Reyes Station
Green Bridge Gas & Auto   (415) 663-8654
Cheda's Chevrolet   (415) 663-1227

Olema
Olema Ranch Campground   (415) 663-8001

BANK / ATM

Bank of Petaluma, Point Reyes Station   (415) 663-1713

CAMPGROUNDS

Point Reyes National Seashore (walk-in)   (415) 663-8054
Olema Ranch Campground   (415) 663-8001
Samuel P. Taylor State Park   (415) 488-9897
Mount Tampalpais State Park (walk-in)   (415) 388-2070
Lawsons Landing (Dillon Beach)   (707) 878-2443

RENTALS FOR RECREATIONAL ACTIVITIES

Bike Rentals
Trailhead Rentals   (415) 663-1958
Cycle Analysis   (415) 663-9164

Kayak Rentals & Tours or Lessons
Blue Waters Kayaking, Inverness   (415) 669-2600
J & M Kayak Adventures, Pt. Reyes Station (415) 663-0333
Támál Saka Kayaking, Marshall   (415) 663-1743
Sea Trek, Sausalito   (415) 332-4465
                                           (415) 488-1000
Stables
Five Brooks Stables   (415) 663-1570
Stewart's Horse Camp   (415) 663-1362

Whale Watching Boat Trips
Oceanic Society   (415) 474-3385

Fishing
Bodega Bay Sport Fishing   (415) 875-3495

WHERE TO STAY

Inns of Marin   (415) 663-2000
Point Reyes Lodging   (415) 663-1872
Bed & Breakfast Cottages of Point Reyes   (415) 663-9445
Inns of Points Reyes   (415) 663-1420
Point Reyes Youth Hostel   (415) 663-8811
Seashore Bed & Breakfast   (415) 663-9373
West Marin Chamber of Commerce   (415) 663-9232
West Marin Network   (415) 663-9543
West Marin Visitor Bureau   (415) 669-2684

WHERE TO EAT

Olema
Olema Farm House   (415) 663-1264
Olema In n & Restaurant   (415) 663-8559

Point Reyes Station
Station House Cafe   (415) 663-1515
Mike's Cafe   (415) 663-1536
Taqueria La Quinta   (415) 663 8868
Point Reyes Roadhouse & Oyster Bar   (415) 663-1277
Cafe Reyes   (415) 663-8368
Joe's Diner   (415) 663-1536

Inverness

Barnaby's By The Bay	(415) 669-1114
Gray Whale Pub & Pizzeria	(415) 669-1244
Manka's Inverness Lodge	(415) 669-1034
Perry's Deli	(415) 663-1491
Vladimir's Czech Restaurant	(415) 669-1021
Knave of Hearts Bakery	(415) 663-1236

Drakes Beach

Drakes Beach Cafe	(415) 663-1297

Marshall

Nick's Cove	(415) 663-1033
Tony's Seafood Restaurant	(415) 663-1107

GENERAL STORES

Inverness

Inverness Store	(415) 669-1041
Inverness Park Groceries	(415) 663-1491

Point Reyes Station

Palace Market	(415) 663-1016
Toby's Feed Barn	(415) 663-1223
Tomales Bay Foods	(415) 663-9335

Olema

Olema	(415) 663-1479

OYSTER COMPANIES

Johnson's Oyster Farm	(415) 669-1149
Tomales Bay Oyster Co.	(415) 663-1242
Hog Island	(415) 663-9218
Point Reyes Oyster Company	(415) 663-8373

BAKERIES

Bolinas Bay Bakery	(415) 868-0211
Knave of Hearts Bakery	(415) 663-1236
Bovine Bakery	(415) 663-9420

NEWSPAPER

If you are interested in keeping informed about local events, political issues, new places to eat or stay consider subscribing to the *Point Reyes Light,* West Marin's *Pulitzer Prize* winning newspaper. Telephone: (415) 663-8404; fax: (415) 663-8458; P.O. Box 210 Point Reyes Station, CA 94956.

GALLERIES

Nearby communities of Point Reyes Station, Olema, Inverness, and Marshall offer a variety of galleries which often feature local artists.

SPECIAL EVENTS

A Sandcastle Contest is held every year on the Sunday of Labor Day weekend.

ABOUT THE AUTHORS

Native Californians Phil Arnot & Elvira Monroe are a perfect team for putting together this comprehensive and highly readable travel guide to the Bay Area's jewel, Point Reyes National Seashore. Arnot is an active and highly regarded mountaineer and explorer. He has hiked extensively throughout California, as well as to regions of Washington, Oregon, New Zealand, South America. Introduced to Point Reyes National Seashore as a child, he has grown up with it as his backyard. He has been dubbed Mr. Point Reyes, and this book reflects his enthusiasm and love for the region. Monroe, a native San Franciscan, is a wilderness and wildlife advocate. Her extensive research and first hand experience will help you explore the wonders of Point Reyes so you can have a complete Point Reyes experience — from its cresting waves to its seaside shops, from its flora and fauna to its diverse wildlife.

Other books Arnot and Monroe have co-authored are *San Francisco —A City to Remember* and *Run For Your Life.*

Arnot has also written *Point Reyes – Secret Places & Magic Moments, Yosemite Valley,* and *The High Sierra.*

Monroe has authored *Walk—Don't Run, Places of Worship in and Around the San Francisco Bay Area, Hawaii – Cooking with Aloha, Greek Cooking for Everyone,* and *Say Cheesecake & Smile.*